LIGHT YEAR '85

LIGHT YEAR
'85

Edited by Robert Wallace
With drawings by Gary Adamson

Bits Press
Cleveland

The acknowledgments on pages 197–198 constitute a
continuation of this copyright notice.

Associate editors: C. M. Seidler, Bonnie Jacobson.

Printed and bound in the U.S.A.

ISBN: 0-933248-03-2
ISSN: 0743-913X

Light Year, the annual of light verse and funny poems,
welcomes submissions. Poems recently published in periodicals
are OK. SASE, please. To:

Bits Press
Department of English
Case Western Reserve University
Cleveland, Ohio 44106

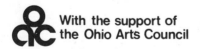 With the support of
the Ohio Arts Council

for E. B. White

COMMUTER

Commuter—one who spends his life
  In riding to and from his wife;
A man who shaves and takes a train
  And then rides back to shave again.

                    E.B.W.

CONTENTS

4

7

1

THE ANSWER IS "NO"

What answer maketh the crow?
Always "No."

Put several questions in a row
To a crow,
You will get "No, no, no,"
Or "No, no, no, no."

Sometimes, on being questioned,
The crow says "Naw"
Or "Caw."
But regardless of pronunciation,
There is never anything but opposition, denial,
And negation
In a crow.

In their assemblies at the edge of town,
Crows introduce resolutions, then vote them down.
How many times in summer, waked early by the
      mosquito,
Have I lain listening to the crow's loud veto!

Once, gunning, I wounded a thieving
Crow
And have not forgotten his terrible, disbelieving
"Oh, no!"

E. B. White

HAZEL TELLS LAVERNE

last night
im cleanin out my
howard johnsons ladies room
when all of a sudden
up pops this frog
musta come from the sewer
swimmin aroun an tryin ta
climb up the sida the bowl
so i goes ta flushm down
but sohelpmegod he starts talkin
bout a golden ball
an how i can be a princess
me a princess
well my mouth drops
all the way to the floor
an he says
kiss me just kiss me
once on the nose
well i screams
ya little green pervert
an i hitsm with my mop
an has ta flush
the toilet down three times
me
a princess

Katharyn Machan Aal

INSPIRATIONAL

We learn something each day we rise from bed;
I'd rather have learned something there instead.

Joachim M. Ardanuy

DISSEVERINGS, DIVORCES

Disseverings, divorces, weddings that went
From woo to woe, from courtship through the courts
—imagine the army of them all arrayed
On some vast ground of neutral reckoning:
No judgment there, but merely memory and dismay
That each of them did love each other once.

Howard Nemerov

THE TRICKLE-DOWN THEORY OF HAPPINESS

It starts in the penthouses, drizzling
at first, then a pelting allegro
falling nowhere except the high places,
and Dick and Jane pull on bikinis
and go boogieing through the azaleas,
and Daddy, ecstatic, comes running
with pots and pans, glasses, and basins
and tries to keep all of it up there,
but no use, it's too much, it keeps coming,
and pours off the edges, down limestone
to the buckets and pails on the ground floor
where delirious citizens catch it,
and bucket brigades keep it moving
inside, until bathtubs are brimful,
but still it keeps coming, that shower
of silver in alleys and gutters,
all pouring downhill to the sleazy
red brick, and the barefoot people
who romp in it, squishing, but never
take thought for tomorrow, all spinning
in a pleasure they catch for a moment;

so when somebody turns off the spigot
and the sky goes as dry as a prairie,
then Daddy looks down from the penthouse,
down to the streets, to the gutters,
and his heart goes out to his neighbors,
to the little folk thirsty for laughter,
and he prays in his boundless compassion:
on behalf of the world and its people
he demands of the sky, give me more.

Philip Appleman

GENERIC POEM

Today was all I could have asked of it—
blue sky and sun present, accounted for;
a mezzotint of sparrows leapfrogging
leaf-bare. An exaggeration, actually.
I could have asked for more—
a sexual encounter of the yet undreamed
of kind (the Indians had it over us there,
a different name for every conceivable position:
"Today, we have the Blue Spruce, Wind-beaten,
Leaning to One Side, the Right, in a Gold Shower
of Leaves and Sun"); any man or woman
toasting Proust: "Here's to Proust!" as opposed
to "mud in your eye" or "us"; a unicorn
trampling Mrs. Jackson's roses that always
seem to win at the Heart of Illinois State Fair.
It's not unlike generic food, which is not
supposed to be all that bad—according to Mrs. Johnson.
As Anaxagoras is said to have observed, "Everything
is everything." What can one do to applesauce?

Ed Orr

JACK BE NIMBLE

Jack be nimble,
Jack be smart,
Snuff the candle
Before you start.

Bonnie Jacobson

from THE BIG CITY MOTHER GOOSE

Little Bo Peep
Lost her sheep.
She went to the local police.
They couldn't find them either.

Tiny Ms. Treat
Stumbled to a subway seat,
Exhausted at the end of her day.
Along came a derelict
Who sat down beside her
& frightened Ms. Treat away.

There was an old woman
   Who lived under a hill.
If they hadn't torn the hill down
   To build a parking lot,
She'd be living there still.

Louis Phillips

AFTER THE PHILHARMONIC

Two paths diverged in a well-known park,
One well-lit, the other—dark.
And since I did not wish to die,
I took the one more travelled by.

James Camp

MORE ROTTEN BRATS

While we dazed onlookers gawk
Baby's borne off by a hawk.
Few, I bet, if any chickens
Ever give it tougher pickins.

*

In the steaming hot tub Kurtz
Surreptitiously inserts
Pirhanas starved till good and mean
Just to help Aunt Jo come clean.

*

Clem with climber's pick and rope
Scales the college telescope
And, height-dizzied, has his vomit
Taken for some novel comet.

*

On his motorbike Lars stands
Roaring past us—"Look! no hands!"—
Soon, with vacant handlebars,
Back the bike roars. Look, no Lars.

*

DEER SANTA:
             GIMME! GIMME! GIMME
ALL YOU GOT.
             YOUR OLD PAL,
                      JIMMY.
(Santa left that greedy kid
Something that a reindeer did.)

*

Emma, eager for a jape,
Lifts the gate latch, lets escape
A roaring bull, which catches Emma
On the horns of a dilemma.

*

Out of roasting pans Felice
Loves to swill her fill of grease.
How she'll squeal when mutton melts!
There's no keeping her in belts.

*

From the fireworks factory Randall
Filched a giant Roman candle,
Took off—whoooosh!—across the dark.
"That lad," leered Dad, "will make his mark."

*

Mom, in bed with friend Ed, screwing,
  Swapping sips from one martini,
Didn't notice Meg undoing
  The stopper, stirring in a teeny
    Drop of seething prussic acid.
    Ed died screaming, "Little bassid!"

*

"Doctor, doctor! Greedy Greg's
Eaten all my Easter eggs!
They were hand-grenades I'd dyed."

"Hmmm," says Doc. "Greg, open wide—
Wider—wider—"
                BOOOOMMM!
                        "Oh-oh.
Guess that's wide as Greg will go."

*

"Great Aunt's evening creme de menthe
Needs," mused Mal, "a boost in strength.
What if I just introduce
This fermented cactus juice . . ."

Dear old Auntie, ripe to die,
Soon was cackling, "Bung your eye!",
Casting an erotic leer
From the crystal chandelier.

X. J. Kennedy

A KIRBY OLSON ADVENTURE CANZONE

Aviator helmut snug, in my Fokker tri-plane
I'm cruising over the board of Monopoly.
St. James Place is bustling. I dip the wing of Fokker tri-
     plane
To say hello. Boss of St. James notes, "Fokker tri-plane."
Am I on reconnaissance? In financial combat?
I will keep my intentions to myself in my Fokker tri-
     plane.
I will keep my lips zipped in my Fokker tri-plane.
I cruise over Boardwalk. I caress the bomb-button.
Bombs spiral through the sky and hit Boardwalk on the
     button.
Anti-aircraft guns sputter at my Fokker tri-plane.
Around my windshield are splotches of green crayola.
Below me is one exploding orange crayola.

Surrounded by puffballs of ak-ak crayola,
I slip through the sky in my Fokker tri-plane,
Releasing my bombs like sticks of green crayola,
Totalling parking lots in flashes of crimson crayola.
Of the skies, you see, I have perpetrated a monopoly.
Birds flutter by sketched in black crayola.
Below the sea is viridian crayola.
On the horizon a lone plane comes to greet me in com-
     bat.
Okay, if it's combat he wants I'll give him combat!
Aerial torpedoes streak from my wing: gray crayola-
Sticks hit the Sopwith Camel right on the button!
It shatters like a mushroom button.

I punch the accelerator button:
Whiz past you like a blurred crayola.
A shirt button pops, it's the neck button.
I must be getting fat, soon I'll pop the next button.
I do a barrel roll in my Fokker tri-plane,

Leaving a dotted line as round as a button.
I wish my girlfriend would unbutton.
It's not fair, her form of sexy monopoly.
I don't ask her to give up all her hotels in Monopoly;
Just want to sleep in one with her and unbutton every
       button.
Why not? I am Kirby the great combat
Aviator: tops at flying and flowery combat.

Are you beginning to think I think only of glory in com-
       bat?
Actually I just like to cruise above the Monopoly
Board. If some fool wants to engage me in combat,
I'm perfectly willing to engage him in combat.
You and I both know I'll turn him into a spatter of cray-
       ola.
Combat! A fleet approaches to provoke me into combat!
O drat! The lead plane is a Fokker tri-plane!
O shit! An entire fleet of Fokker tri-planes!
Hired by Boardwalk to defeat me in combat.
Those rich blue suits have monopolized Monopoly.
But I am the skymaster: secret genius of Monopoly.

I will destroy them in the name of Monopoly!
Tri-plane by tri-plane I will splatter in combat
Over the motley map of Monopoly!
Gently I push an anonymous button:
Prussian blue crayolas smash their monopoly.
Three Fokkers streaming green-crayola smoke plummet to
       Monopoly
Inferno, while my magnificient Fokker tri-plane
Serenely annihilates a fourth catatonic ochre Fokker tri-
       plane.
It is I who claim the Sky of Monopoly!
Pardon me, but with my Fokker tri-plane
And superb handling I could destroy any old Fokker tri-
       plane.

Ah, but it's getting dark out so I land my Fokker tri-
        plane,
To sleep in a new hotel on Pennsylvania Ave. Monopoly
Is a lovely sport, but sleep, that delicate combat
In my brain, is silent as a gray button,
Until the morning sky of a blue crayola.

Kirby Olson

PIERCING THE SLOT

CLEAN & EASY TO USE
Pierce Slot with Knife
Made in England

—from the label on a bottle of
    Stephens Economical Spreader Gum

Oh, a Nipponese knife
is convenient of course
to commit hara-kiri
when filled with remorse,
and a blade made in Mali
will skin you a goat,
and a dirk from Dalmatia
will stab you a throat,
but even James Bowie
would agree, like as not,
with those good folks at Stephens
whose gum we have got:
        Pierce slot with knife
        made in England.

Knute Skinner

SOME RIVER RHYMES

Racing on the Firth of Forth,
I tacked West instead of North;
I came in last, not forth or firth—
A day I should have stood in berth!

*

Sailing down the Kill Van Kull
I hit a rock and stove my hull;
I listed port, I listed starboard—
I darn well wished that I was harbored!

*

On the Hudson, up near Nyack
I met an Eskimo in a kayak.
He shouted out, "I'm lost. D'you know
How in heck to get to Juneau?"

*

Sailing on Penobscot Bay
Someone hollered, "Ship ahay!"
"No, no," I said, "it's 'Ship ahoy!'
Go back to port, you stupid boy!"

*

Sailing on the wide Sargasso
I caught some flotsam with my lasso;
My companion tried to get some,
But managed just to get some jetsam.

*

Sailing on a Norwegian fjord,
I was getting rather bjored,
So I asked our captain, Bjorn,
To play Sibelius on his hjorn.

*

". . . where Alph, the sacred river, ran,"
Coleridge wrote, in "Kubla Khan" . . .
Oops! He stopped, he heard a door knock,
It was that bloody man from Porlock!

*

When sailing on the Brandywine
I leap about and frolic;
The Brandywine's my favorite stream—
It's so darned alcoholic!

*

On my boat on Lake Cayuga,
I have a horn that goes "Ay-oogah!"
I'm not the modern kind of creep
Who has a horn that goes "Beep beep."

*

I've heard about the river Dee,
And there's a river Wye, I see;
What river has more letters yet?
The sacred river Alph I bet!

*

Drifting out on Walden Pond
My brow began to furrow,
Those candy wrappers on the shore
Would thoroughly displease Thoreau!
(As for that sodden paper cup—
The sight would make Thoreau throw up!)

*

Whilst we were sailing on Loch Ness
We spied a water monsteress;
She took a dive—we couldn't catch her—
She looked a lot like Margaret Thatcher!

*

Sailing off Cape Hatteras
The waves began to batter us,
One hit the ship so very hard
It rolled me off my matteras!

*

Sailing on Lake Calumet
Thinking of a gal you met
Long ago, in this same Michigan—
You never will meet such a dish again!

William Cole

HOW OFTEN MANET GENUFLECTS

National Gallery, April 1982

How often Manet genuflects
To soft sweet napes of women's necks,
While Renoir, painting, here directs
Our gaze to peach-fuzz frontal sex.
No matter, rear view or façade,
For both I thank a loving God.

Ray Bradbury

SOUND ADVICE

Vivaldi said, "Mr. Scarlatti,
Our music sounds terribly spotty.
I get thoroughly bored
At this dumb harpsichord,
Man, its jangles are driving me dotty."

Said Scarlatti, "I, too, am tormented,
But I beg you, dear sir, be contented.
I dread what I think'll
Become of our tinkle
When once the piano's invented."

Vivaldi replied, "I take pride in
The way our horizons can widen,
But the keyboard is strange
And we're too old to change,
Let's leave that to Mozart and Haydn."

Rhoda Bandler

FRED ASTAIRE, WHERE ARE YOU
WHEN I NEED YOU?

Though many aspire to excel at romance,
The pearl beyond price is the man who can dance.
I'd happily overlook faults
In one who had mastered the waltz;
Both murder and mayhem would shrink to mere flaws
If only he'd practiced his one-two-three, pause.
Since I am a fox who can trot,
I'd teach him both twist and gavotte,
And think him an ace of a fella
Should he try a gay tarantella.
He'd never need fear my attention would flag
Performing the Charleston or lindy or shag;
I could do without macho or muscle
If he could but tango or hustle—
His beard could be curly or wiry
If just his fandango were fiery—
He could be French or Danish or Polish or Scottish
Provided he'd rhumba or polka or schottische.

Hannah Fox

DO GO ON—I COULDN'T BE MORE FASCINATED

I don't know what intrigues Frenchmen, Italians, Bel-
        gians, or Danes
But of all the boring subjects that interest Englishmen the
        most pervasive is trains.
Among my male acquaintances it's more popular than
        football or cricket,
Though as a topic of conversation I've never known a
        woman to pick it.

Questions about life and love and human nature are the
ones we like to kick around
But a man would rather discuss what year the last steam
train ran on the London Underground.
If I were a lesbian separatist or a nun
I'd probably be unaware that the answer is 1961.
The men in the office are an indefatigable source of infor-
mation
About everything from the Orient Express to Crystal Pal-
ace High Level Station
And when the one at home says, "Darling, there's some-
thing I really want to see on BBC 2"
I ask wearily, "Has it got wheels? And does it go choo-
choo?"
And, sure enough, we eat our supper watching an old
engine with nothing special about it
Roaring through a landscape that would look much more
beautiful without it
While some wally drones on about the excitement and ro-
mance of the age of steam
Until I want to do what I did when I was very small and
heard a train coming, namely cover my ears and
scream.
Still, we all have to count our blessings and it's only fair
to say
That train buffs are really quite amiable and harmless and
even the history of Acton Central is preferable to
"Match of the Day."

Wendy Cope

FOOD FOR THOUGHT

In primitive societies, tribal warriors used to believe that by devouring the heart of their bravest adversary, they could bolster their own courage.

Unlikely as it seems, this theory has now received some astonishing support. By grinding up planarians—inch-long, leaf-shaped flatworms—and feeding them to other planarians, University of Michigan psychologist James V. McConnell discovered that the cannibal worms suddenly began displaying the behavioral responses of their dead, devoured brothers.

—*Newsweek*

> Lemon or sugar, sour or sweet,
> I owe what I am to what I eat.
> Chicken or rabbit, lion or lamb,
> I owe what I eat to what I am.
> Teataster, beefeater, vegetarian,
> Rosicrucian or Rotarian,
> Inch-long cannibal planarian,
> Being what I am, to be complete
> Or just to be at all I eat.
> In a nutshell, then, in an epigram,
> As I am, I eat; as I eat, I am.

William Jay Smith

ODE TO GARLIC

Sudden, it comes for you
in the cave of yourself where you know
and are lifted by important events.

Say you are dining and it happens:
soaring like an eagle, you are
pierced by a message from the midst of life:

Memory—what holds the days together—touches
your tongue. It is from deep in the earth
and it reaches out kindly, saying, "Hello, Old Friend."

It makes us alike, all offspring of powerful
forces, part of one great embrace of democracy,
united across every boundary.

You walk out generously, giving it back
in a graceful wave, what you've been given.
Like a child again, you breathe on the world, and it
     shines.

William Stafford

TRADITION AND THE INDIVIDUAL TALENT

An old-school foxhunter let it get around
that he hunted a deer-proof pack. Hard to believe:
foxhounds are born to run foxes, all right,
but you have to make them stay off rabbits,
housecats, chickens, etc. They learn to stop
when the hound-whip cracks. Deer scent, though,
is strong enough to put whips out of their minds.

So, somebody asked, how do you do it?
Take a bag of deer scent and a hound,
put them both in a fifty-five-gallon oil drum,
and roll it down a hill or a rocky road.
God almighty. You claim this really works?
Seems to. One thing I'll say's for damn sure:
they stay away from fifty-five-gallon drums.

Henry Taylor

TO AN ATHLETE RETIRING YOUNG

When some coach found you in the rough
and said you had Olympic stuff
if you combined a life of training
with anchoritical abstaining,

you glowed with adolescent pride
and set all other thoughts aside
to dedicate your waking hours
to sweaty gyms and freezing showers.

From High to U., from State to Region,
the challenges you met were legion.
You won each prize you could procure
and still remain an amateur,

until the banner was unfurled
in that stadium where all the world
could watch you win your golden cup.
From this there was no higher up.

So now, with trophies on the shelf,
the time has come to store yourself:
a golden idol under thirty
encased in glass cannot get dirty.

An uncle wants your fame to bring
eclat to retail marketing,
but Father thinks your clean-cut face
should grace a senatorial race.

Your sister says your physical fixtures
were really made for motion pictures,
but Mother would much rather see
those charms used in the ministry.

Though each of these conflicting voices
depicts a future full of choices,
you settle on your only sport
as court of first and last resort

and with a sigh at last approach
your high school for a job as coach
so you can fill young heads with glory
and others can replay your story.

Judson Jerome

BORG, BORG, BORG

*Lines Composed After Viewing a Tape of the 1980 U.S. Open
Men's Final in Tennis on CBS Television*

Break, break, break,
   Of the cold stony-eyed Swede!
And my tongue can not help but utter
   The thoughts that arise in me.

O well for the Summerall boy,
   That he shouts with Trabert at play!
O well for the Newcombe lad,
   On the court with his mike for good pay!

And the stately serves go on
   Though Open and Slam are uphill;
But O for the touch of Bjorn Borg's backhand,
   and a victor with a voice that is still!

Bitch, bitch, bitch,
   Every foot of the way, McEnroe!
But the tender grace of a champion
   Is something you still do not know.

                              Doyle Wesley Walls

EXERCISE IN PREPARATION FOR A PINDARIC ODE TO CARL HUBBELL

               Long after, Carl,
You will be fabulous: may my song show how!

If but our culture were less disunited,
A poet such as I, "young and promising,"
Might hope to know so great an athlete . . .

O Carl! I saw you once go into Loew's,
After you lost 1–0 to Paul Dean,
And wished to say, Tough luck, Carl Old Boy!
But the words choked in my throat—
                  How many times
From Coogan's Bluff as from the walls of Troy
Have I not gazed between the crevices
Of the upper and lower grandstand down below,
In desperate interest and open fear
That a short single would break up the game!

—Spring, immoral Spring, is now upon us,
And in my twenty years of tense devotion

To the great Giant cause, this is the worst
Spring I remember. Bill Jurges, racked
With headaches, on his way to Mayo Clinic,
Terry without a shortstop! But worst of all
The power of the Dodgers who so long
Competed with the comic strips,
                                    Alas, Babe Herman,
Ototototoi! Ototototoi! you who once tried
To steal second with the bases loaded!

Delmore Schwartz (1959)

TO THE HAM-HANDED ORGAN PLAYER WITH AN IMPROVISATION FOR EVERY OCCASION AT MCCORMICK FIELD, HOME OF THE ASHEVILLE TOURISTS:

How I love them
ball-park Francks!

Michael McFee

NIGHTGAME

Empty and alone after a nightgame, Comiskey Park looms
like Brontosaurus over the south side of town, the
power cut to nothing, a sky gone dark as friction tape,
the moon unplugged. Waxflower beer cups already going
        to seed
litter the playing field like souvenirs of some other age,
cover the sod with lingering statistics in the standings
of what once was. Now the scoreboard registers another
        game,

suspended in emotion. The spectre rounding 3rd as fleet as
     moonlight
is the Cuban White Owl, Minnie, sliding safely home, pri-
     mordial
in his ease. Phantom drives are driven into darkness
from the batting cage, limned upon the night as frozen rope.
One is lost up near the towers, lighting up the dark, then
plummets, falls to earth a captive of the cosmos, swallowed
by a nebula encircling the upper deck where one fan always
     sits alone
amid a cloud of smoke with his cigar and panama. Con-
     suegra rocks
inexorably in the bullpen below, untouched, immortal, his
motion mesmerizing, 16–3 till the end of time. Around the
     cage
the chatter is intense and meteoric. Sherm and Bubba, pick-
     ing lint,
watching as Jungle Jim pulls a shot into the right field alley,
lean on their bats, looking long and hard. In the wake
of drives that clear the fence they ponder things Pythago-
     rean
as an afterthought: Who will take the measurements along
     Andromeda
for reddish shift, where do orbits end and start, when shall
     undreamed
quantities be known, how to solve Narleski in the ninth?

Ron Ikan

2

THE ROCKETTES

Now when those girls, all thirty-six, go
to make their silky line, they do it slow,
so slow and with a smile—they know
we love it, we the audience. Our
breaths suck in with a gasp you hear
as their legs in casual unison
wave this way then, and that, and their top
hats tilt in one direction,
and their sharp feet twinkle like a starry row
as the pace accelerates, and the lazy legs
(thirty-six, thirty-six, what a sex
to be limber and white and slender
and fat all at once, all at once!)
that seemed so calm go higher, higher
in the wonderful kicks, like the teeth
of a beast we have dreamed and are dreaming,
like the feathers all velvet together
of a violent contracting that pulls us in,
then lets us go, that pulls us in,
then lets us go; they smile because
they know we know they know we know.

John Updike

CONTEMPORARY SAINTHOOD, POSSIBLY

A principled lady who wouldn't sell to the Ramada Inn,
But retained her house to stand cornered by the Inn
      grounds
Like a touching historical monument almost engulfed
By the usual graceless high-rises that haven't stood long
      enough
To be called historical—
                this lady of principle—
Raiser of flowers, assiduous feeder of birds—
Said of those multiplying imports, house sparrows and
      starlings,
(Graceless barbarians that assimilate and are not
      assimilated)
When they swarmed to her feeders: "Well, I'm not
      Miss America,
But I get just as hungry as she does."

That's a version of sainthood, I guess. Saints are
      principled do-gooders
Who love the masses, it seems, but don't love
      individuals.
(More speed to Thoreau, who said that if he found out
Someone was approaching him to do him good
He'd run a mile) . . .
             Be all that as it happens to,
And greatly as one may respect courage and
      principle,
I wish house sparrows and starlings would all fly away
And flutter round saints, to make them feel more
      saintly,
And leave me with one pair of chickadees.

W. R. Moses

ANTIQUE BLUE CHAMBER POT

Antique blue chamber pot
pride of her collection, placed
centerfull of pears bananas and
green grapes. My, how
Sam Johnson would have stared.

Edward Willey

THE EDWARDIAN LADY

Alone in her mansion utterly bored,
The Edwardian Lady pulled a bellcord:
To the tinkling of a distant bell
Down from the ceiling a tapestry fell
Depicting the Saints in the torments of Hell—
Saint Catherine, Saint Barbara, Saint Teresa, Saint Joan,
Saint Eulalia pounding on walls of stone—
And out stepped a man, who, with consummate ease,
Won the Lady's confidence by degrees,
Until, without a distasteful word,
He swept her off through the chestnut trees
In a crayfish net filmy and wet,
On a journey the Lady will never forget
And dumped her, far from the tinkling bell,
Unceremoniously into a well.

When the candles bloom on the chestnut tree
And they set the crumpets out for tea,
Janie, the maid, and the butler, Henri,
Hear through the delicate filmy air,
Up from the drive and the porte-cochère
To the tinkling of a distant bell,
The sound of a saint in the torments of Hell,

The voice of a Lady utterly bored,
And the echo of her strange ennui,
The echo of her strange ennui.

William Jay Smith

EPITAPH FOR A STRIPPER

Rose LaRose now seeks repose,
Her soul stripped to the buff.
To God's she turns from clapping hands,
Now we have seen enough.

Richard Goldsmith

EPITAPH FOR
AVID DIVA

She crossed a continent of scales,
From C to shining C.

Michael McFee

MY SISTER

After the funeral of her
husband, a lewd and filthy
inventor who dies leaving
her without a cent,
she dries her handkerchief
on the radiator and reflects,

"All I have left is my soul,
and of course, my body, both
wrapped in the same thin paper.
Of the two, my body seems
more important, perhaps
because I'm hungry and out of
Pepperidge Farm and apricot jam."

Dressed in a magenta robe, her feet
bare, she takes the M. T. A. to Harvard
Square, where she begins to hop about,
banging a tambourine, chanting,
Soul for sale! Sale on soul!
and other catchy slogans. But strollers
and joggers act as if her soul

is invisible as air or angels.
On the first day she collects thirty-
two cents in her begging bowl,
and decides to sell her body instead.

Phyllis Janowitz

PINK PANTSUIT

It hangs around the wardrobe
for days, dull,
or reclines in the hamper

like a flattened flamingo.
I wash it in soft water.
I give it new life, and what thanks?

It walks out the door
through the gate
headed straight for the racetrack.

Nancy Simpson

MY DAUGHTER THE COLLEGE FRESHMAN

My Daughter the College Freshman
thinks I have a good mind if you can
find it underneath years of PTA,
Brownies and Christmas shopping.

My Daughter the College Freshman
thinks women are treated as sex objects
and must resist; me too, even though I
may not look like a sex object.

My Daughter the College Freshman
thinks it's time I knew Zen and Shinto are
Eastern philosophies and not last names,
or don't I care what people are thinking?

My Daughter the College Freshman
says cooking and cleaning are not her thing
and she will never, never do them, even though
it was nice I did them when she needed them done.

My Daughter the College Freshman
doesn't know my mother calls me every week
to ask why my daughter the college freshman
doesn't comb her hair and put on some decent clothes
and settle down, or don't I care what people are
thinking?

Rochelle Distelheim

GRADING

"Grading's no problem. An experienced teacher can grade anything."

—An experienced teacher

He grades the cat on being cat
(straight A), the grapefruit on juiciness
(B+) and sweetness (B), his wife
on sleeping soundly (last night, D
−); he grades the morning (C
+, *be more definite*), the dog
for coming quickly when it's called
(A−, *good dog, good dog*), for
fetching the paper (*Fetch it!*—F).
In broad daylight he grades the moon
last night at midnight, *Well defined,
clear, and complete* (pure A, pure A);
his breakfast lunch and dinner (Pass);
his shoes (Unsatisfactory);
of course he grades the morning paper
(low C for content, C for form);
the window (B, maybe B−,
try to be more imaginative).

He grades the way he drives to school
(B+ *woops*,D), the radio—
rather, its choice of music (A
+, for Segovia's guitar
followed by Goodman's clarinet),
the fat opossum in the road
(plain D for *dead*), the old man trudging
in red sweatsuit and jogging shoes
(Not Pass), the parking lot (OK),
colleagues for cordiality
(A, B, C, D, none of the above)
and courage in the line of duty
(withheld: cf. the Privacy Act).
He's graded God (*You should do better
than this, with Your Advantages.
Try to improve by putting more
of Yourself into it*, C−);
and *homo sapiens* (*barely passing*,
YOU ARE IN TROUBLE!);

                    and himself
(Delivery, B: Coherence, C;
Organization, D; Good will,
A! A!), and grades his grading (C,
inflated, whimsical), his life
(B+ *as far as it goes, keep going*),
tomorrow and tomorrow and
tomorrow (*Where's your outline?* C,
no, Incomplete. *Please see me soon.*)

John Ridland

LIFE'S UPS AND DOWNS

Vicissitudes are often met
   At every crossroad, every mile.
But ups and downs do most beset
   The moviegoer on the aisle.

Marcy S. Powell

POEM FOR A NEW CAT

Watching her stand on the first
joints of her hind legs like a kangaroo
peering over the edge of the bathtub
at my privates floating like a fungoid lilypad,
or her bouncy joy in pouncing on a crumpled
Pall Mall pack, or the way she wobbles walking
the back of the couch, I think when
was it we grew tired of everything?
Imagine the cat jogging, terrified
that her ass might droop, or studying
the effective annual interest paid
by the First Variable Rate Fund, the cat
feeling obliged to read those poems that
concentrate the sweetness of life like prunes.
O.K., that's ridiculous—though the cat
also kills for pleasure—but I find
myself in the middle of the way,
half the minutes of my sentient life
told out for greed and fear.
The cat's whiskers are covered with lint
from the back of the dryer.
               Friend,
how it is with you I don't know
but I'm too old to die.

Ed Ochester

THE CLUMSY MAN

Well, I am clumsy. I stumble, I hit my head
on chandeliers. I'm a tall, clumsy man.
I miss my mouth with my food, I fall out of bed,
I forever bite my cheek or else my tongue.

The woman I love has learned to be wary near me
lest I turn suddenly and put my elbow
into her teeth or deep in her dear kidney.
We kiss and my forehead knocks against her brow.

Unless I am careful, careful, careful, careful,
I drive over the curb or crack my wine glass.
I have tied my left shoe to my right
and dropped a baby. All of it will pass.

When the choir sings over my perfumed bones,
I will cough until I am asked to leave.
I will step on my undertaker's toe,
lurch through his oak door and, farewell, feel

sweet symmetry around my open wings.

Richard Frost

THREE MORE FROM THE ARABIAN NIGHTS

Three Kalandars* and their Tales

I

Know, O my brothers, that like you I am
a kalandar and eunuch, though I was once
First Wazir to his Majesty the Caliph,

*a kalandar is a hobo.

Akmar Hasan Ashkenazi, The Terrible and Wise.
I wear a size nine eye patch and occasionally
scratch what is left of my once famous cullions,
that now take up an entire corner of The Wise One's
study, along with my eyebrows, a foot, and
my body's good hair. About the Caliph's third wife
don't ask; The Wise One took more pity on me.
But you there, kalandar number two, I see
that you wear a patch and a rag upon your
misfortune; friend in misery and travel,
tell us what happened to you.

II

My story is so bizarre that even you
will not believe it, but by The Dugs
of Allah, here is the truth, good kalandars:
Many years past I was daughter to a caliph,
who said of me, "Her navel would hold an ounce
of the finest ointment." And I worshipped him
more than the great Allah himself, but when
I heard he promised me to the first Wazir,
I tore the hair on my head and clawed my breast
and prayed that Allah would take me, but instead
he sent a Jinni, who turned me into a comely
young man, then vanished before my father came upon
me in this state and spat in my face when I
told him the fate of his daughter. For my trespass
he cut off a foot, my new testicles, then took
my right eye with one fillip of his finger.
Later, when his daughter couldn't be found, he
had a filthy blackamoor shave my head, who swore
I was uglier than he before he cast me
out the window. But what of you, third kalandar?
Is your story more unusual than that?

III

Yes, my castrated friend, unusual is not the word,
for I was once, at the same time, the lowest

and highest thing on earth, one of three turds
laid in a fragrant forest by a great caliph, who
for a joke told the Jinni of the forest to turn
me into a wild swine, for he had strayed from a hunt
that had so far proved fruitless. The Jinni did this,
for he knew the power of the king, but when he saw me,
cowering and shaking, unused to life, and the caliph
hacking away at my cloven feet, and you see for yourself
what else he did, the Jinni turned me into a human
being, and the king took pity and left without a word.
The spirit restored my right eye, gave me this sturdy
walking stick, and by the Grace of Allah brought me
here to you, my blessed kalandars and friends, but
let me tell you what I heard along the way, which
is even more miraculous.

Roger Weingarten

ABBÉ DE BRANTÔME IN PRAISE OF LEGS*

to A.B.

There's such excitement in a leg,
Foot to ankle, calf to thigh.
Women would be well-advised
To think how Vito knelt to beg
Melind to turn away her eyes
While he removed her silver shoes.
The first of many things she'd lose.
It's wise to keep one's legs exquisite,
Preparing for a similar visit.

*Brantôme was a sixteenth century French courtier. In 1583 after a serious fall from his horse, he retired to his estates to write Viedes dames galantes, a humorous account of the sexual life of the nobility.

Royal Henri rode a chilly mile
In freezing mist from Lyons to Bains.
His blood was burning all the same,
On his face a simple smile,
Gone leg-mad, quite leg-insane.
For his flush he was in debt
To a sweet nymph of the royal fete.
Little tunic, scalloped hem.
An eyeful worth his diadem.

In ballet we know it's the legs
That make men crowd the concert halls.
Lust will wink at curtain calls
for *pas de deux* not worth two pegs.
So why do legs attention beg
From poets warm for curls and lips?
Praise Beauty's pattern, toes to hips!
I love the ladies' other parts,
But legs are shaped to break men's hearts.

Mary J. McArthur

A LITTLE MUSIQUE IN 1661*

When Twenties gramophones were tinny
and girls were shaking it in mini
immodest skirts
with bathroom gin, bootleggers, mobsters . . .
who knew that you *did eat two lobsters*
or cared? It hurts

to think how history behaves so flightily—
my head, you noted, *akeing mightily*
from *pints of wine,*
The Pillers of Hercules, The Goate
keeping your Navy men afloat—
where they could dine

on *chine of beef* and *leg of mutton,*
burnt-wine and *sack,* that every glutton
supped like a whale,
new-come-to-town North Country bugger
nine-pinned by *Rhenish wine and sugar*
or *cups of ale!*

They also gave some frightful wallops
to platters full of *eggs and collops,*
to eat an *udder*
was commonplace, although the thought
does not entice us as it ought,
but makes us shudder.

*All the phrases in italic in this poem are taken from the famous Diary of Samuel Pepys in its most recent full and unexpurgated edition, the work of R. C. Latham and W. Matthews. Pepys was a Civil Servant (as we should now say in Britain), working for the Navy Office. In 1661 he was 28, ambitious, hard-working but fond of pleasure—this included food and drink, plays, looking at pretty women in the streets and theatres, and music. He played the **flagelette** (flageolet or flute) and sang in a bass voice. A **wigg** is a cake or bun (a cookie in America). **Collops** are pieces of fried bacon. **The Pillers of Hercules** and **The Goate** are two of the pubs where he entertained the visiting sea captains; another was called **The Legge**. The **Gitterne** was an early member of the guitar family. **Bugger** has to be pronounced in the British North Country way, to rhyme with **sugar**. The whole poem is addressed to Pepys himself by the writer.*

One friend did tell, and made *much sport,*
Describing *his amours at Port-*
smouth to one
of Mrs Boates daughters; a kitten,
a pretty girl play of the Gitterne,
to hear—what fun!

In clover cloven hoof, hot pig!
So thinking there *to eat a wigg*
you late came home—
a dish of Anchoves gave you thirst,
fuddled perhaps, you never burst,
each chromosome

was *very merry with the ladies,*
though sermons gonged of Hell and Hades,
your *morning draught*
was standard, *barrels* too *of oysters,*
both fore and aft,

kept you shipshape and in good case.
Your *flagelette* (and you sang bass)
was womanlike
in giving you and others pleasure;
good time, good tunes, proportion, measure,
no marlinspike

could separate melodic strands
(like piano pieces for eight hands)
when *ayres* were woven;
brave echo banged a bastinado,
opiniastrement, rhodomontado,
and pre-Beethoven!

Music was food—and you had cause
to love the art that Henry Lawes
practised divinely;

not reckoned by the frivolous, you
worked hard at what you had to do,
and did it finely.

Gavin Ewart

FABLE

Franklin sailed a key-hung kite
And watched the storm-stung flight of it.
Everyone seemed much impressed—
But Edison made light of it.

James Facos

DEWEY DECIMAL

Thomas Dewey had great political acumen
And ran for president against Harry S Truman.
George Dewey sank a whole Spanish flotilla,
Became admiral and was the hero of Manilla.
John Dewey's pragmatism was most impressive
And he made our public schools progressive.
But all these feats are really infinitesimal
Compared to Melvil Dewey and his famous
    Dewey Decimal.

Library of Congress call numbers phooey,
Give me the decimals of Melvil Dewey.

Raymond Griffith

CLERIHEWS

Catherine of Aragon
was probably no paragon,
but she couldn't have been ruder
than Henry Tudor.

John S. Robotham

John Keats
As a child loved big teats.
When he got to be a man he
Preferred Fanny.

George Gordon, Lord Byron
Was pursued by an Italian siren.
But he thought it more chic
To go Greek.

Percy Bysshe Shelley
Thought all fish smelly
And never learned to swim—
Unfortunately for him.

R. A. Simone

Claude Monet
Painted stacks of hay,
But they gave him the willies,
So he switched to lilies.

Margaret Blaker

James Bond
Should have been drowned in the pond
When he was a kitten
Before he got written.

Richmond Lattimore

CAESAREAN SECTION

Cesare Borgia
Would have preferred the situation in Georgia
Before the Emancipation
Proclamation.

William Harmon

STILL LIFE

Albert and Victoria
Were never renowned for public euphoria;
They must have been much like we see 'em
In the wax museum.

Paul Humphrey

TRIPLE CLERIHEW: A QUESTION THAT IS NEVER ASKED IN THE EXECUTIVE SUITE OF DOUBLEDAY & CO., INC.

If Nelson Doubleday
ever troubled a
Jackie Onassis
to attend the night classes
of Samuel Vaughan
do you think she'd yawn?

David R. Slavitt

●59

CLERICAL CLERIHEWS, OR, A BEGINNER'S GUIDE TO PATRISTICS AND BEYOND

Saint Paul (?–67?)

Saint Paul
Explained it all
Except the thistle
In his epistle.

Saint Simeon Stylites (390?–459)

Saint Simeon Stylites
Didn't have any nighties;
"But that's all right," he said,
"I don't have any bed."

Miguel Serveto (1511–1553)

Miguel Serveto
Picked up a hot potato
When he questioned the Trinity
In Calvin's vicinity.

Joseph Smith (1805–1844)

Joseph Smith
In concert with
The Angel Moroni
Wrote a lot of baloney.

Martin Buber (1878–1965)

Martin Buber
In his "Ode to a Tuber"
Wrote, "Ach, mein Kartoffel Kind,
Du bist, ich bin, wir sind!"

Scott Bates

A GOOD MANTRA IS HARD TO FIND

I forget the difference
Between karma and dharma;
I may say the latter
When I mean the pharma.

My mantra's a mystra
That's better kept mum;
When I say OM, sistra,
I'm thinking *homme*.

Margaret Blaker

ANOTHER POOR SOUL

> ". . . we do not know how long individual
> souls are detained in purgatory."
>
> *Baltimore Catechism*
> *November 19, 1952*

If I die in venial sin,
I go to purgatory:
not as good as heaven,
a lot better than hell.
I'll stay
until the people still alive
can pray me out.
I imagine being one prayer short.
A hundred years go by
because everyone forgot
or thought I already made it.

Ed Engle Jr.

BISHOPS

Bishops have flat hair
and very long earlobes.
They wear hats shaped like trowels,
and tomato-colored robes.

Bishops stroll between
limousine and steeple.
They always call their subjects
sheep instead of people.

Bishops carry crosiers
that make a sound like brass.
They never cross their knees
when they are running Mass.

Bishops wear white gloves
to tap on children's cheeks.
They say when they say no
it's God himself who speaks.

Bishops live long lives
and rarely say perhaps.
They have no sins to speak of
and take extensive naps.

At length it's heaven where
bishops' names are shipped.
The rest of them is packed
in mothballs in a crypt.

Mark McCloskey

LE PAPE DANS SA PISCINE
(a partially found poem)

What do you think of these photographs?
L'audace des photographes c'est un scandale.

Why does the Pope engage in physical culture?
*Le Pape est obligé de pratiquer la culture physique
pour combattre l'arthrite.*

What does the Pope do before he dives in the pool?
Il se signe avant de plonger.

What else does he do?
*Avant de plonger, le Pape fait le signe de la croix
et s'arrête un instant pour méditer.*

Does he stay in the pool long?
*Le Pape traverse plusiers fois la piscine
en nageant puis revient vers l'échelle après le bain.*

And after his laps?
La séance de natation est terminée.

Then?
Le Pape sort de la piscine avant de se diriger
vers le vestiaire.

He wrings out his own suit?
En pantalon et tee-shirt blanc le Pape essore
son maillot de bain puis il quitte la piscine.

Anything else?
La séance de natation est terminée.

Sue Standing
(with help from *Paris Match*)

GOD AND HIPPOPOTAMUS

In the beginning God said to Hippopotamus:
Kiboko, I want this bank kept clean.
Your job is to keep the grass in line.

Kiboko answered the Lord saying:
Your will is my command, but please—
may I loll the sun-hours in the stream?

God thought deeply upon the matter; finally
he said, All right, I suppose—
just don't be eating all the fish.

Now every night Kiboko mashes clay
between her hooves. When she goes
she shits and pisses both at once,

her tail a propeller, scattering the mess
up and down the twilit bank,
distributing it for God to examine.

See? she says, her billiard-ball eyes
rolling up to the moon—
no scales.

Michael Finley

RITUAL, ANYONE?

a lil ritual l
sumtimes gitchoo
a hole lotta
pompan
circumstanz,

sumfanzy
pranz-n-
stanzin,
aweebidda
seek-cure-ity

in obsess-'if'
repet-ishun,
azyoo trade
a pawn trad-ishun,
an snatchdabatch

yawl figger
soochoo bess.
so mebbe yawlotta
sikh hi wotta,
nodoodah tranz-danz,

hang titan hierundnau,
anstai vizuelle.
foriffa stitchin
nein saves thyme,
aniffa schu fitzhugh,

don't be-wear it—
ware it! bud, real eyes,
ederway yugo, hugo,
money-rit-u-al
nevvagit!

Russ Traunstein

MICKEY'S PILLOW

> "A friend of mine (Mickey) made me
> the most wonderful pillow: it's 2 moose
> mooning in a marsh in the woods."
>
> —from a letter

2 moose mooning in a marsh in the woods
must mean more than at first appears.
Many mottled mangoes mashed within their mouths
might indicate a morbid reason for their tears.

Moose mainly meander into marshes when confused
and munch on mint or mistletoe or other freaky fruit
moodily moping, never giggling or amused.
Some mimic the mandolin or mouth organ or flute.

2 Sioux sunning on a sward of snow,
swinging skillets, smiling, should set your heart aglow,
but 2 moose mooning in a marsh in the woods
must be murky omens and up to no goods.

May Swenson

OPENING DAY AT NEOPARK

For authenticity,
The singing of birds,
The undulations

Of squirrels, are programmed
To happen at random—
Lifelike. From flower

To flower (accuracy
Simulation 98%)
Electric bees navigate;

Water the brook gurgles
Is real. The tourists enter
To gape at historic nature.

By a papier-mâché madrona,
The custodian watches
Through plexiglass eyes.

The antenna behind his ear
Quivers. Grinning,
He slowly runs a thumb

Along the blade of his hoe.

Michael Spence

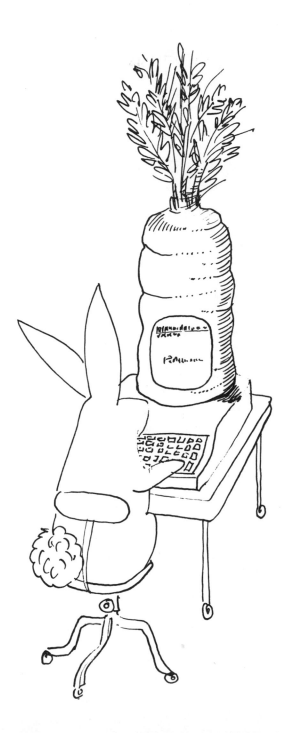

3

LETTER TO ORANGES

For days now I've watched you grow fat,
And you changed completely the way you sat.
You rested your belly upon the floor
And your voice meowed endlessly, "More! More!"

First of all, you're not my cat.
But today I didn't think of that.
I heard a cry and I rushed in the door:
You'd had five kittens upon the floor.

The rest of the afternoon I sat
And looked at you, such a beautiful cat,
And wondered if I too sat on the floor
And meowed endlessly, "More! More!",

Would your handsome master make me fat,
And could I too change the way that I sat?
And later on could I lie on the floor
Purring proudly, happy, and sore?

I could never be such a graceful cat.
Easier for you than for me to grow fat.
But girl or cat, some ancient lore
Makes us both cry, "More! More!"

Delmore Schwartz (1946)

THE MATERNAL INSTINCT AT WORK

In the bed Dinah curls,
kittens tumbling over kittens
at nipples pink and upright
against the silver blue fur.
Her mrow interrogates.

The second night she toted
them one by one into my bed
arranged them against my flank
nuzzling, then took off
flirting her tail.

Birthing box, bottoms
of closets, dark places,
the hell with that. She
crawled between my legs
when her water broke.

Think of them as *ours*
she urges us, have you
heard of any decent daycare?
I think kitten raising
should be a truly collective

process, and besides, it's all
your fault. You gave me
to that little silver
balled brute to do his will
upon me. Now look.

Here I am a hot water
bottle, an assembly line
of tits, a milk factory.
The least you can do
is take the night feeding.

Marge Piercy

SHORT NOTE ON A CAT SLEEPING

for Nancy

a sleeping cat hears every sound
you once told me

today the november wind rattles
the window glass
& I watch a cat sleeping
grey paws upturned
a leg buried beneath his thorax
like a knot of silk
his tufted ears waiting

I toss an empty beer can into
the waste basket
& not a whisker twitches

how nice
after all this time
to think of you & how you lied
to me about everything
including cats

Stephen S. Smith

ON PERSPECTIVE

It's not just a question of what they say,
But also of who is "they."
When cannibals speak of a gourmet dinner,
They mean that they ate a gourmet.

Roy Blount Jr.

OH, SHOOT!

I saw some birds upon a roof
And thought I'd take a shot.
A photograph, I mean, of course—
A hunter I am not.

I chose an f-stop carefully
For proper depth of field,
Adjusted shutter speed to match,
The perfect snap to yield.

I held the camera up and aimed.
Nope—needs a longer lens.
Put on my telephoto zoom
And focused once again.

Set up the tripod—musn't shake!
Fixed filter, screwed on shade.
And just before I took the shot
The critters flew away.

Jeanne Munn Bracken

BREAKFAST FOR TWO

My old dog is eating waffles
sloppy with butter & syrup.

I always set a place for him,
he likes to eat with me.

I ask him if he wants more:
the old dog licks his chops & says yes.

Another & another, 8 more before he sags
to the floor, sighing, maybe thinking:

the last batch was the best ever.

Michael Snow

IT'S SPRING, SPRING IN PITTSFIELD, MASS.

It's spring, spring in Pittsfield, Mass.,
    Track and slide go bare;
It's raining hard in many a pass,
    And balmy blows the air.

The thaw has come to Pinkham Notch,
    It's forty-nine in Stowe;
Up, crocus, up! Come, slip, come, vetch!
    We'll sprout before we go.

It's slush, slush in Intervale,
    The ski is on the rack,
The snow train threads the greening dale
    With sun upon its back.

It's spring, spring in Montreal,
    Laurentian lads are hot;
Old winter on his knees shall crawl.
    I say, "Why not, why NOT?"

E. B. White

FERNS

The Marsh Fern, the Wood Fern, the Pond Fern,
The Japanese Painted Fern, a multicolored frond fern,
The Interrupted Fern, an easy to discern fern,
The Boston Fern, a pedestal and urn fern.
The Fishtail Fern, the Oriental Brake Fern,
The Massachusetts Fern, or Bog Fern,
The New York Fern, the Silver Leaf Fern,
The Brittle Bladder Fern, the Log Fern.
The Walking Fern, a tip-propagating fern,
The Mother Fern, a self-duplicating fern,
The Climbing Fern, the Beach Fern, the Cliff Fern,
Ebony Spleenwort, which is a very stiff fern,
The Male Fern, a traditional vermifuge fern,
The Mexican Tree Fern, an absolutely huge fern.
The Bird's-Foot Fern, the Bird's-Nest Fern,
The Ostrich Fern, the Feather Fern,
The Hen-and-Chickens Fern, the Hedge Fern,
The Felt Fern, the Leather Fern.
The Christmas Fern, a bright evergreen fern,
The Spinulose Shield Fern, a very seldom seen fern,
The Marginal Shield Fern, a spores along the edge fern,
Sierra Cliff Brake, a grows upon a ledge fern.
The Rabbit's-Foot Fern, the Hare's-Foot Fern,
The Squirrel's-Foot Fern, the Claw Fern,
The Elk's-Horn Fern, the Hart's-Tongue Fern,
The Deer Fern, the Bear's-Paw Fern.
The Royal Fern, a likes it moist and shady fern,
Like Goldie's Fern and the Northern Lady Fern,
The Resurrection Fern, a revives in the rain fern,
The Broad Swamp Fern, the Virginia Chain Fern,
Mrs. Cooper's Lip Fern, a grows where it's dry fern,
The Shasta Fern, a likes to live high fern.
The Petticoat Fern, the Verona Lace Fern,
The Button Fern, the Cloak Fern,
The Venus-Hair Fern, the Ribbon Fern,
The Locust Fern, the Oak Fern.

The Staghorn Fern, a tree-dwelling air fern,
The Bristle Fern, the Delta Maidenhair Fern,
The Sensitive Fern, a deeply indented fern,
The Licorice Fern, the Common Hay-Scented Fern.
The Skeleton Fern, the Rib Fern,
The Holly Fern, the Ladder Brake Fern,
The Five-Fingered Fern, the Hand Fern,
The Wart Fern, the Rattlesnake Fern.
Bracken, a knows no enclosures fern,
The Grape Fern, a grows without croziers fern,
The Cinnamon Fern, a florists' give-away fern,
The American Shield Fern, another bouquet fern,
Purple Spleenwort, which is really a blue fern,
And the Asparagus Fern, which is not a true fern.

Raymond Griffith

TRANSFORMATION

Mike leaves his Honda
In the spring rain. It will grow
Into a Buick.

Janet Ruth Heller

SUMMER SCENE

A meadow in majestic green
    Spreads out before my eyes;
Delightful rolling hills recede
    Into the distant haze.

Along a tree-lined winding brook
  Some horses run and caper,
While cows and sheep graze happily—
  What beautiful wallpaper!

Pier Munn

A BETTER BIRDHOUSE

Planning a house for the martins
I was about to begin it
when one flew close by and seemed to say
they'd like a bathroom in it.

Darrell H. Bartee

CREDO

Last fall and through the winter
a woodchuck minded the woods
behind the house, in coarse but
amiable conformity to type.
I watched him strip a dozen
weeds of foliage, enter and leave
his burrow, waddle, sprint,
and glide like a Russian dancer.

Then we found an opossum
grubbing in a garbage can at dusk
one day this spring. It was smaller
and less lively, but when lifted
by its tail showed its teeth.
We let it go. The woodchuck,
meanwhile, seemed to have moved on.
His replacement glowered like a demon.

This summer only a skunk has been
coming around. Rabid skunks
have been caught outside of town,
but this one looks perfectly happy
and hasn't bothered a thing.
Naturally I'm beginning to suspect these
changes are due not to succession
at all, but metamorphoses.

In fact, that's what I firmly believe.
There's nothing that says we won't soon
see a hippogryph, minotaur, or man
emerge from the treeline
to forage in our garden.
I'm setting bait—olives, cheese,
and falernian wine—hoping Ovid himself
appears some evening, clothed in leaves.

Dan Campion

CENTIPEDE, MILLIPEDE

A one-bug Rockettes, the centipede
Choreographs its kickline front to back
Too quick for the eye to catch, its drunken track
A desert adaptation to mislead.

The millipede prefers it rich and dank.
Two legs per segment instead of the centipede's one,
Its delicate platoons of dancers run
On pointe over twig and pebble like a tank.

The millipede is a kind of flowing dart
Lubricating precisely through unctuous loam.
Devious, blond and dry as its desert home,
The centipede has won my insect heart.

Bruce Berger

THE ENGINEER

Sharks, ranging in size from a few feet to monsters rivaling the mechanical star of Jaws, can attack in cold or warm waters as shallow as 18 inches. They can detect sound over a mile away and pick up a scent from a half-mile. Their division is superior to humans'.

Daily American, August 12th

Not only can he hear and smell
as if with radar, and as well;

As through the man-infested tides
this prodigy of purpose glides,

His mind is not beset by whims
of dainty, dancing, dangling limbs

But by the problems they present:
refraction, density, ascent.

Bruce Bennett

THE POWER OF INSTINCT

At Rancho Nuevo, on the smooth beaches
of Mexico's eastern coast,
when the time comes to lay eggs
the Kemp's Ridley turtle always returns
to the same sands it first touched as a hatchling.
Even when biologists take it far away
it swims thousands of miles, back to the same spot.
And there it lays its eggs
and then lies panting, looking around with beady eyes.

Frankly, I am not as impressed as the biologists.
Years ago in a coin shop
I met Bill Hadley of Beachview, Ohio.
No matter how far away he may be,
on a golf course, or in a bar, or at a wedding,
he unfailingly returns to the same branch of Central Bank
on the precise day his certificates mature.
And his eyes glisten
as the new zeros are typed on smooth, fresh paper.

P. K. Saha

WEREWOLVES

Yes, my children, there really are
shaggy creatures who walk at night, their teeth
seemingly tinged with blood. But do not believe
the legends that have them sipping dew from a wolf's
footprints, or cringing under a magic spell.

Science tells us they merely suffer (for suffer they do)
from a tragic lack of enzymes, which leads to a build-up
in body tissue of prophyrins, making their skin painfully
sensitive to light. Hence, they tend to be hirsute
and stay inside during the day, with drawn shades
and covers pulled over their heads. Their reddish grins
are another sign that something's not right.

At sundown they rise and wander sadly through a pale,
hostile world, sobbing or even wailing a little.
(Wouldn't you?) It is not true that they eat bad
boys and girls (rodents, perhaps, an excellent source
of enzymes), nor that by saying their real names—
Mr. Frost! Aunt Mabel!—you can return them to normalcy.
Nor would I advise hitting them three times over the head
while making the sign of the cross. They need affection

and understanding, just like the rest of us, and the
    company
of their own kind, e.g., Werewolves International.

If you see one in the park, don't be scared. Act natural.
Should a love affair develop between you, I suggest
counselling, prayer, tests, and a basement apartment.
Should you detect in yourself alarming symptoms—
hairy arms, a pink toothbrush, the need to jog after dark—
stay calm. Science is finding ways to save us all.

Jane Flanders

NIKSTLITSLEPMUR

(For Caeri, my 4-year-old daughter,
who said, "Let's read it backwards tonight.")

The dwarf sprang cursing
from the ground,
then smiled and danced.
The queen said, "Mot, Kcid.
No, Sgelredips, or Rapsac."
But she finally resigned herself
to stuffing her child
back into her womb.
Then she quit the king
for a tower
where the dwarf gave her a ring,
a necklace, and rooms full of straw
from gold.

Then her father, the Miller, said,
"Straw of out gold spin
can who daughter a
have I."
Then they were poor and unhappy,
normal.

F. Richard Thomas

LINCOLN'S CHIN

On a big green field
We ran for Easter eggs
If it had a picture of Lincoln on it
You got a bag of jelly beans
If it had George Washington on it
You got a chocolate Easter egg
The man wanted my Lincoln
I wouldn't give it up
He wouldn't give me the jelly beans without taking the Lin-
    coln
I decided that Lincoln was better than jelly beans
While I was talking with the man
My brother who hadn't found anything
Stole eight bags of jelly beans
Ate them all himself
I ate my egg
After failing to keep Lincoln's face uncracked
I saved the piece with his chin
I knew the rest anyway
I still have the chin
My brother still remembers throwing up jelly beans

Jim Finney

BALLOON MAN

He sells his breath
In shiny rubber bags.
They call him concession-

Aire.

Charles Ghigna

BEAR MALLING

A little mall went up
Near a wooded glen
And Momma Bear went shopping
To decorate the den

Papa strolled to Sears
To look at fishing poles
Sister ran to Pet World
To price the baby moles

And Junior on a quest
To find himself again
Went to Waldenbooks
For paperbacks on Zen

Charles S. Evans

TOM TIGERCAT

Tom Tigercat is noted
for his manners and his wit.
He wouldn't think of lion,
no, he doesn't cheetah bit.
Tom never has pretended
to be something that he's not.
I guess that's why we like him
and why he likes ocelot.

J. Patrick Lewis

FOR FUN

A horse and a cow
and a great horned owl
sang in a voice like one.

With a neigh and a moo
and a who who who
they sang, they said, for fun!

So a cat and a dog
and a fat pink hog
sang in a voice like one.

With a hiss and a howl
and a grunt from the sow
they too said oh, what fun!

In the barn, in the field,
with a wondrous yield
they sang in a voice like one.

With a neigh and a moo
and a who who who,
with a hiss and a howl
and a grunt from the sow
they sang, they said, for fun!

Roger Pfingston

THE OWL

Though I don't wish to seem too fanatical,
I consider the owl ungrammatical.
"To-whit, to-who" he sits and keens;
"To-whit, to-*whom*" is what he means.

Robert N. Feinstein

LITERALIST

R U A B I C?
O O U R A B!

John Fandel

SOME CRITTERS

The Azbit

He has to run, trot, lope, sprint, gallop, or anyhow
      keep going,
owing

to being oddly designed:
one leg way in front, the other way behind—

so that, like
a bike,

if he isn't whizzing, this rover
just topples over.

When he gets tuckered, he
has to lean himself against a tree.

The Razor-Tooth Gnore

A most ferocious carnivore,
the Gnore

(as it happens) also makes
the most delicious steaks.

Hunters of the Gnore are sometimes the winner,
and sometimes the dinner.

The Merry Cuth

A spider the size of a snow,
the Cuth loves for the wind to blow,

wiggling little legs like lightning.
One, of course, isn't frightening,

but when they party or swarm,
it's a storm.

The Oo-oo

Having a head
at each end, instead

of only at one, the Oo-oo has two fronts
and so faces two ways at once.

He's double smart;
but also troubly at the start—

for his predilection's
to galumph off in both directions.

The Zing

Since splitting in two's
how microscopic folk reproduce,

the family of the Zing
is puzzling.

One Zing unzips into two, the two into four,
and soon there are millions more,

all kin to each other,
but no one's a father, mother, sister, brother,

and of course there can't
be gramp, cousin, uncle, aunt.

All Zings must be, ancestrally speaking,
one and the same Zing.

Robert Wallace

AN EXPERIMENT IN SLANT RHYME

Some thieves sacked the home of Miss Hughes
Who owned a remarkable nose.
She said, "Sirs, I shall sneeze
And alert the police
If you don't get out of my house."

Wesli Court

WOOLLY WORDS

The spine has been tingled; the horn has been swoggled.
The blood has been curdled; the polly's been woggled.
   The mind has been bent, and the heart has been rent;
   The pan has been handled; the ambi is ent.
The polysyllabics have got the mind boggled.

So fiddle the faddle while whimming the wham
And cater the corner while flimming the flam.
   The ki has been boshed, the hog has been washed,
   The gast has been flabbered, the buckles are swashed,
And here is a boozle in search of its bam.

The tara's been diddled; the kum has been quat.
The fili's been bustered by Hotten the tot.
   The horn has been piped, and the tin has been typed;
   The knick has been knacked, and the gutter's been sniped,
So hiero the glyphics and poly the glot!

Robert N. Feinstein

MY CUP OF TEA

I often lose my cup of tea
walking from room to room.
I do not know why this should be.
I often lose my cup of tea.
I have a good forgettery.
I also lose the spoon.
I often lose my cup of tea
walking from room to room.

Lillian Morrison

CAT

Cat's out of the bag.
That's what we heard
at the lunch counter.

Of course we don't
know what the cat is
in the first place.

Now, there must be
some valuable cat
roaming around.

Collect all the cats.
Have a line-up. Are
you the cat that got out?

Eric Linder

OUTSIDER

"Come in," said the keeper,
"Come into the zoo.
Our cages are lacking
a creature or two
and possibly one of those
creatures is you."
"Not me," said the Dodo
and winked.
"I'm extinct."

Emily Otis

A JUMBLE OF BIRDS

Phoebe Gannet, bittern booby,
grouses towhee nightingale,
finches, ducks a throated-ruby,
falcons dove with mountain quail.

Chickadee from Carolina
snipes at heron Phoebe's breast.
"Auk!" she hawks and crows, "It's myna!
Ptarmigan to tern the nest."

Toucan love but one can nary—
Phoebe's gone stork raven mad.
Grackles like a cassowary,
"Ibis all aloon and sad!"

J. Patrick Lewis

OYSTERS IN LOVE

Some people think oysters devoid of emotion,
But this is a wholly erroneous notion.
When female meets male in the group known as bivalve,
The very first question is: "Your valve or my valve?"

Robert N. Feinstein

THE CAT, THE MAID, AND THE GENTLEMAN

Hevera, devera, dick:
Eight, nine, ten—
That's how they count their sheep,
These Westmorelandmen.

A maid and a cat lived in a sty,
   (The Devil you know dwells down below),
A gentleman came and caught la eye.
He stopped and stared and wondered why
The maid and the cat lived in the sty,
   Hevera devera fo la fo.

The cat and the maid were eating eggs,
   (The Devil of course dines down below)
And dancing about on barrels and kegs.

The gentleman asked if it hurt fo legs
To be dancing about while eating eggs,
  Hevera devera fo la fo.

The maid and the cat were smirched with dirt,
  (The Devil wears ashes down below).
"No," la replied, "it does not hurt
My legs if I keep my prancing curt
And cover myself with lots of dirt,"
  Hevera devera fo la fo.

"La, marry me," the gentleman said,
  ("The Devil will marry us down below.")
"I'd be most pleased if we were wed
At midnight, be we quick or dead.
I'll marry thee merrily, sir," la said,
  Hevera devera fo la fo.

They were betrothed eight days all told,
  (The Devil was waiting down below),
La and the gentleman so bold.
The deveral sun set dark and cold,
And they were wed as the church bell tolled
  Hevera, devera, fo, la, fo.

The cat (not maid) and the gentleman were
  Wed by the Devil down below.
Listen and you may hear fo purr
(Not la, for who could care for her?)
The couple are gay, or at least they were,
  Hevera devera fo la fo.

Wesli Court

4

STICK MAN WITH FRUIT AND VEGETABLE

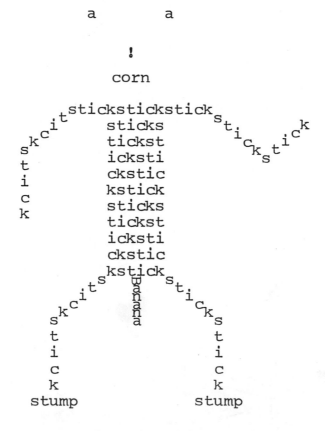

Jay Dougherty

ET IN ARCADIA EGO

Shepherds, I have got the clap,
  Possibly from Phyllis.
Fate, the Author of Mishap,
  Bred me this bacillus.

Distillate of Mercury
  Spreads its royal tincture
On the fallen parts of me,
  Just below the cincture.

To the purple lately raised,
  And immodest glory,
Let me hereabouts be praised
  As your *Re Pastore*.

Anthony Hecht

L'ART

Your clothes a dark pink heap, a dimming sky,
I bite the inside of your mocha thigh:
Matisse preferred to paint this scene, not I.

Frederick Feirstein

CUPID'S QUIVER

I shot my seed into the air
It landed here, it landed there
I know it's not the thing to do
But, Valentine, I thought of you

Bruce Bennett

THE SPELLING BEE

In sixth grade I won a spelling bee
with *cadaver*. I wrote it
on the blackboard, the teacher
smiling by the open door. Her lips were red
and later, after school
when I imagined kissing her in the cemetery
she kneeled and unbuttoned her white dress.

I thought how every grave must be a bed
moving under us.
I wanted to lie down beside her
in the silk of a coffin. I wanted
the whole class to lower us down,
their little fists
pounding like hearts to get in.

Jack Driscoll

THE FETISHIST'S LAMENT

To what increased effect, when placed like this
In an inkwell, her braids appear, the blond
Hair of a sudden black! It knits a bond
Between us, myself and my dear miss,
Her inky tresses soliciting my kiss,
Making my fingers ache with sweet despond
Because the scissors glisten there beyond
My reach. What joy it would have been, what bliss
To snip these glories from their golden crown
And fly them flapping from the handlebars
Of my red Schwinn! O what a blessed bike!
I'll do it yet—I'll make her hair my own!
Did Berenice's braids mount to the stars?
So shall my queen's, when I do what I'd like.

Tom Disch

DEATH OF A VIRGIN

All during school we studied her. Life's joys
Are common to all men, but not the same
For each of us: maybe a thousand boys
Jerked themselves off while muttering her name.

Howard Nemerov

THE UNRUINED MAID

I was a virgin when I married;
My mother called it security;
I wish now I had not tarried,
Such were the wages of purity.

James Camp

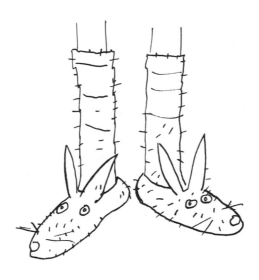

TOTAL ABANDON

I thought it was just a casual fling.
But I knew, when I looked in my eyes
it wasn't purely physical,
I loved me for my mind too.
At first, I played hard to get.
Love's not worth anything
if it comes easy.
Sure, I could have plied myself with alcohol,
got me into bed,
but I'm not that kind of guy.
I respect me.
This isn't some Saturday night two-step,
Sunday morning shuffle out the door.
This is for keeps.

Carl Rosenstock

MORALITY

All during dinner he nearly lost himself,
Whenever she leaned forward, looking down
The deep Vee of her loose unbuttoned shirt.
If anything could make him think, that would,
And to such effect that later on that night,
Having looked her down, he decided to look her up.

There was no phone book in the motel room.
So he got her from the Gideon instead:
Her number was PRoverbs 5 3456,
Extension 727. So that was that.

But later, as he laid him down to sleep,
He thought how all good children go to heaven,
While as for all the other children, well,
Strange woman . . . and wondered would he ever cease
To wonder at the consternation could be caused
In a perfect stranger by a couple of bumps in a blouse.

Howard Nemerov

THE LOVER NOT TAKEN

Committed to one, she wanted both
And, mulling it over, long she stood,
Alone on the road, loath
To leave, wanting to hide in the undergrowth.
This new guy, smooth as a yellow wood

Really turned her on. She liked his hair,
His smile. But the other, Jack, had a claim
On her already and she had to admit, he did wear
Well. In fact, to be perfectly fair,
He understood her. His long, lithe frame

Beside hers in the evening tenderly lay.
Still, if this blond guy dropped by someday,
Couldn't way just lead on to way?
No. For if way led on and Jack
Found out, she doubted if he would ever come back.

Oh, she turned with a sigh.
Somewhere ages and ages hence,
She might be telling this. "And I—"
She would say, "stood faithfully by."
But by then who would know the difference?

With that in mind, she took the fast way home,
The road by the pond, and phoned the blond.

Blanche Farley

SINCE I WOULD NOT STOP FOR DEATH

Since I would not stop for Death,
That Cad, he stopped for me.
I told my maid I'd waste no breath
On such a one as He.

From upper window through a crack
I saw His car draw near;
He drove a big black Cadillac
That opened in the rear.

I noted He was dandy-dressed—
Top hat, tails and studded cane,
But beneath that Sunday best,
I knew He was no gentleman.

At first He knocked quite civilly,
Smiled and said, "My card—
Would you go tell Miss Emily,
I'll take her for a ride."

This speech was *all* off-color;
I cannot be too hard.
Color may rhyme with dolor
But never *ride* with *card*.

He shouted up, "WILL YOU COME DOWN!"
I said, "Quite frankly—No.
I'd not give You the run-around—
It's not my time to go.

"My labor—and my leisure too—
Have made my schedule tight.
I've got a lot of work to do:
Not all my rhymes are right."

Then flash, He did His courting dance.
The things He did I cannot tell;
I got a little tiny glimpse
of what they do in Hell.

He drove so fast past every star,
He took my breath away—
There was another in that car—
Miss Immorality.

Not to preach behavior here;
But if we reach Infinity—
'Twill burn the Blessed Savior's ear
When Death and I part company.

James Camp

WILDERNESS ENOW NOW

A liter
of Perrier, a wedge
of Camembert, and thou beside
me on the quad,
ducking frisbees.

Jim Elledge

APPLIED BEAUTY

Glory be to God for sexy things—
   For cries of coupled lovers as they bind and bow;
     For moles that on her hip'll make his dolphin swim,
Fresh and fired-up; nutty balls; G-strings;
   Lovescapes pulsing and flesh-shoaled—furrow and plow;
    And all shapes, their leer and freckle and whim.

All people dumpy, bald, regressive, strange;
   Whoever is fickle, faithful (who knows how?)
   With slick, abrasive; sweet, tart; disheveled, trim;
Who father-forth and mother-forth all change,
     Praise him.

Dabney Stuart

NORTHERN LIGHTS

Farmer Manosh liked his beer
and small reputation for turning
a phrase among intimates, their knees
situated under a game of chance, mugs,
and pipes filled with smouldering

dark Virginia leaf. At midnight,
July, sixteen hundred
and ninety-one, he rose
from the bench to relieve himself
under the Milky Way in a trench

behind the bakery. When he turned
away from the business at hand, a woman
with auburn hair appeared, by candlelight,
to be pressing currants into a cake.
Tea breads rising along the walls

like miniature coffins in a mausoleum,
he quickly entered the humidity, and,
with moderate success, after
lifting her apron and dress, after lowering
several more or less distinguished

undergarments, he was having his cake,
when, with a primitive
whale bone rolling pin, she began to smooth
the wave of his hair fallen over the red
eruption of his nose

to the cove at the rear of his cranium.
Outraged, he withdrew to the local
constabulary's chambers, complaining
of an assault, gratuitous and nearly
the end of his game, by a Mistress

Goody of York—handed up before His Honor
and fined an amount appropriate
to her crime. Whether
she paid, willingly, or refused in favor
of having her ankles and wrists locked

into the stocks while Manosh and neighbors
circled around her solitude,
everyone, in a hundred and fourteen
variations on the outcome, tells
a story of a different color. If she paid

(1) in the coin of the realm, did Manosh
have a vision become legend
over dice and ale and passed like a Bible
through generations, where Goody
came to him white as flour and wearing a pastry

apron that she begged him to taste;
or,
if she chose (2) the humiliation,
did he swallow his tongue and almost
die under a cloud-covered

sliver of moon? If you chose (1),
it is the last thing you remember;
if (2), dress warmly and go immediately
to (3); if you can't decide,
or refuse to cooperate, give us a tale

about a hermaphrodite escaping on ice skates
from enemies on Lake Champlain. (3):
Goody's arms surround Manosh tobogganing
under an ice-covered pine that bridges
Snow Hill. She introduces a thin blade

of sunrise to the third and fourth vertebrae
of his winter coat. Near the foot
of the hill, she tumbles into the point
and their blood
becomes the aurora around the heart of the whole

world without end. Amen.

Roger Weingarten

THE GIRL WITH THE SHY SMILE

The girl with the shy smile is holding a quarter.
She is holding it out toward you.
In her other hand is a chocolate bar, with nuts.

Between the two of you lies a wooden counter,
and you are standing behind it.
This will go far to explain the girl's behavior.

Well it isn't enough for you to take her quarter,
and it isn't enough to return her shy smile.
You must tender her her exact change.

And of course you must let her leave your shop
with the chocolate.

Knute Skinner

NEXT MOVE

It's a dangerous game,
sitting so close:

high stakes
no rules

and are you playing?

Bruce Bennett

TRAVELER'S AGENT

Cradling a swan-white telephone
in the curve of her Leda-lovely neck
but bussing the moment's silence mauve
with her country-store placebos and asides
("where there's life there's hope")
she confirms at last my space
in the sullen clabbered sky.

While her sweetcream smiles—ripeness
bursting decolleté et ceteris paribus—
lure clichés to a thousand deaths,
her "life-hope" oracle sounds right,
suddenly, above the news of crashes
blackening this morning's paper.
Dare I ask:
What hope may an inter-Olympian loper,
booked out of this cornfield office,
out of these ice-cream mounds,
dispatched to the dairy sky, curd to whey,
entertain if he returns
(according to the myth) alive?

A. L. Lazarus

HEELS THAT WOULD NOT STOP
AS AN INVITATION TO LUST

(after Miró)

The diamond smiles at dusk;
stars effect a false humility.

Her heels were so high her head
was in the clouds. Little wonder
he felt inadequate, a saucer
without cup, eraser without lead,
who considered rope and pulley,
extension ladder, scaffolding,
the human cannonball trick,
a helicopter. "A bit dramatic,"
he thought. Still he loved her;
and when she began to sing,
he knew the opera was over.

Ed Orr

LEGALESE

An attorney, when asked to pre-pay
By a girl in a thin negligee,
    Said, "It's more fun *pro bono*."
    To which she said, "Oh, no.
For that, you can do it *pro se*."

Hubert E. Hix

DINNER DATA

When a damsel's
Out to dine
With her dinner
She has wine,
But she's learned
(To feel impassioned)
She should down
A chic Old Fashioned,
Or else relax
Without her hat on
In amber glow
Of a Manhattan.

Dick Hayman

ITALIAN RESTAURANT

"You look," she laughed, "like an Italian restaurant!"
Meaning my flickering neon sign,
My massive menu? "No, just your shirt . . ."

(Checker-tablecloth red and white.)
But later she noticed the mandolin music,
The glowing goblets of Valpolicella.

Barry Spacks

CRICKET POEM

Swerving right at the corner of
Bay Ridge and Melrose,
I grabbed a crippled five-legger
as he stumbled the Dodge floorboard.
The other ninety-nine crickets,
purchased for fish bait at Barlow's,
spilled from their coffin
into Saturday sunlight
and scurried off beneath
dash padding and seat backs.
I sat with the car door open,
that five-legged jiminy tapping
encyclopedia into my palm,
and wondered what ninety-nine
crickets could do to a Dodge.

Nancy Simmons and I went
down that night with the *Thresher*
deep into the sea-green back seat
of that fifty-three Dodge.
Off Chinquapin Round Road
the news died whining on the car radio
and I pleaded like a doomed sailor.
She was about to moan yes
when a cricket whispered in her ear
and another called from
the glove compartment.

Suddenly her sisters were singing
in sun visors,
her mother cajoling from beneath
the clutch plate,
her father screaming in the dome light,
cousins chittering in the heater vents,
neighbors gossiping behind
the dashboard,
the cricket tabernacle choir singing
in ninety-nine part harmony
Nancy Nancy Nancy Nancy
save yourself forever.

Stephen E. Smith

JUMP CABLING

When our cars	touched
When you lifted the hood	of mine
To see the intimate workings	underneath,
When we were bound	together
By a pulse of pure	energy,
When my car like the	princess
In the tale woke with a	start,

I thought why not ride the rest of the way together?

Linda Pastan

GOOD TIMING

The full wet wind
and how we rushed to put on our slickers
banging the door and shoving
past each other to get to the car.

We were laughing and pulling hoods
down over each others' faces
while rain hit the windshield
like pellets but didn't stop us.

At Alley's Store
empty of people
all produce available
I bought three boxes of mallomar cookies
and we stocked up on popcorn and soup.

We were glad the rain didn't stop.
That would have been bad news, I think.
We ate, the warmth of the fire spilled out
and then in the morning
the sun was up.
Good timing.

Joan Halperin

FAT LENA AND MR. M.

The young girls flit and flutter, trying
   to brush the cold from the house,
they cut his hair, sew pink and purple pajamas,
   or make a set of glasses from old
beer bottles, the color of the sea.

But only fat Lena cooks, *coq au vin,*
   pumpkin soufflé, plum tarts topped
with nutmeg and cream, and the house
   smelling of garlic and cloves
and fresh bread rising and apples baking.

She watches Mr. M. as he eats,
  becomes a crumb dancing on the waves
in his mouth, slides
  down his throat and licks her lips
with a rather thick tongue.

Mr. M., O eat me too,
  she sings at the stove,
I will be married in the fall.

The dog barks at her shrill voice
  but he loves
Lena and the crisp skin of roast duckling
  she feeds him, basted with oranges
and ginger;
  and sometimes the delicate
                    fromage gourmandise
that Mr. M. brings home
  for his favorite dumpling.

As he nibbles her apricot ear Mr. M.
  is so safe from the cold,
because fat Lena is the winter
  for him now and snow

the melting point of her white skin
  in front of the fire as she licks
his fingers as if they were
                    lozenges,
  and he slowly devours her
      like a giant white
                    wedding cake,
      topped with pink roses.

Phyllis Janowitz

WHAT SUE KNEW

When Great Aunt Sue,
  6 foot 2,
married Theodore,
  5 foot 4,

the family said,
  A blunder.
But now they're all
  6 foot under,

proving what Sue
  always said—
Horizontally, nobody
  beat Ted.

Bonnie Jacobson

TWO MODERN MARRIAGES

1. The man who married Cassandra
   (Who generally was right)
   Had a tendency to meander
   In and out of sight.
   I-told-you-so's are cheesy,
   So how could she exult
   When what he said would be easy
   Turned out difficult?

2. The woman who married Cupid
   Found it hard to believe
   He could be so damned stupid:
   "*Have* you taken leave
   Of all your bleeping senses?"
   She'd ask him as he stood
   Naked of all pretences
   Like Phallos in a wood.

John Ridland

SUMMING UP

If God were married He would know
The devil has a case also.

Joachim M. Ardanuy

A NOTE ON LIBRARY POLICY

We should never have opened the stacks to the undergrad-
    uates.
It's become their favorite trysting place. Like crafty Abe-
    lards,
They hide their fingers underneath their books
And pluck at Héloïse.
They swarm; they kiss in cubicles; for all we know
They breed down there in the twelfth century.
(That's where the bulbs are broken; the stack boys
Have to use flashlights on that level.
But they never report anything amiss—
Sworn to secrecy, probably.)
It's most distracting.
How is one to annotate his bibliography
When everywhere he finds these naked couples
Hiding deep in darkened carrels?

I know. They try to be quiet.
But every now and then a girl will laugh;
Warm and moist,
The sound floats up between the cracks of the neoclassic
    shelves,
And when one is trying to correlate variant versions—
Well, really.

Larry Rubin

REVISION

Juliet
Was wrong:
Parting sucks.

John Bicknell

STRANGE CORRESPONDENCE

Strange correspondence have we had,
Yet he would be a liar
Who claimed to read a single word
I now commit to fire.

So, Lucy, do the same with mine:
Let all go up in smoke!
They'll call us lovers, doomed, divine . . .
(And we can share the joke.)

Bruce Bennett

SHALL I COMPARE THEE TO THY ASTON MARTIN?

Shall I compare thee to thy Aston Martin?
Thou hast a quicker pick-up and ignition.
Oh, engineers are still in kindergarten
puzzled by the design of thy transmission.
Compared to thee, thy elegant *coupé*
might park in stables and subsist on silage.
Thy dash has dials in luminous array
recording greater speed and better mileage.
Not fuel injection, no, nor carburetor
could formulate that essence, sweet concoction,
that keeps thee running earlier and later
and longer, when thy heap has gone to auction.
  Thy beauty wrenches cannot make nor mar,
  and even sonnets may outlast thy car.

Judson Jerome

STRUGNELL'S BARGAIN

My true love hath my heart and I have hers:
We swapped last Tuesday and we felt elated
But now, whenever one of us refers
To "my heart," things get rather complicated.
Just now, when she complained "My heart is racing,"
"You mean *my* heart is racing," I replied.
"That's what I said." "You mean the heart replacing
Your heart my love." "Oh piss off, Jake!" she cried.
I ask you, do you think Sir Philip Sidney
Got spoken to like that? And I suspect
If I threw in my liver and a kidney
She'd still address me with as scant respect.
Therefore do I revoke my opening line:
My love can keep her heart and I'll have mine.

Wendy Cope

Please.

Paul Ramsey

SOME RIBALD RIVER RHYMES

Punting on the River Cam
With my pretty popsy, Pam,
I said, "Pam, let's park this punt
And have some fun, you silly   girl!"

*

Sailing on the Bay of Biscay
I thought of something rather risqué,
And turned to all the ladies, quipping,
"Hey, let's all go skinny-dipping!"

*

We did it in the Strait of Dover—
I thought our loving must be over—
But when we reached the Bay of Cardigan
I found that I had gotten hard again!

*

Sailing Juan de Fuca Strait,
Admiring my gorgeous Kate
Serenely puffing on her hookah—
Any man would Juan de Fuca!

*

As we were sailing the Mianus
I said to dumb, but lovely, Janice,
"Janice, dear, now don't be heinous
And mispronounce this stream 'Mianus'!"

*

On the shores of Gitche Gumee
The maid Nokomis whispered to me,
"I'm thorry now I ever let you—
Hiawatha good girl till I met you!"

William Cole

R. I. P.

At the condom's funeral,
it was reported,
the whole family turned out:
Saranwrap,
gloves for surgeons,
shower caps,
garbage bags,
an infield tarpaulin,
even
some dirigibles.
But if anybody wept,
it didn't leak.

Philip Dacey

RHINOCEROS POEM

Rhinoceroses are becoming extinct.
Poachers are killing them by the thousands for their horns.
Rhinoceros horns are very valuable on the black market.
Why are they so valuable? Because of sex, of course;

Because of macho old men and the one thing they dread
Which is sex failure. Fiasco. Not getting it up.
Rhinoceroses are powerful, their horns are stiff and hard,
And when ground into powder and mixed with lots of other
    stuff

They are swallowed by doting old men who think they can
    become potent again
In spite of the fact that, scientifically, the whole business
    doesn't make any sense.
Yet if they think they can, sometimes they can:
The powder occasionally works as a restorer of confidence.

But it lets you down fast. Which basically proves a vast,
    horny lack of imagination in the world,
An idiot inability to take life simply as it comes
And move with Rhinoceros grace through complicated jun-
    gles of muscle and nerve
Making love with everything you have, rheumatic ears and
    elbows, arthritic knuckles and thumbs

In elemental equatorial delight. Because, after all, who wants
    to go to bed anyway with a worried old man?
Generations of women have proved that sex can be re-
    warding and a lot of fun too
If you aren't drinking Rhinoceros juice by the gallon and
    hung up on whether or not you can
And forget about being a conquering hero and start doing
    what is most enjoyable for both of you to do.

So men, especially wealthy old men who can afford to buy
    Rhinoceros horns,
Take it easy. Relax. Stop acting like such horses' asses.
Make love with what you have: you'll get many more happy
    returns,
And she'll like you all the more and you'll save the Rhi-
    noceroses.

Scott Bates

●119

READING AS AN INTRODUCTION TO CYCLING AS AN INTRODUCTION TO . . .

I had never thought of the bicycle as anything
so erotic until I read of it, in Richard Church,
"that the little nuts and nipples joining the spokes
to the rims shone like jewels." But come to think
of it, the forward thrust and poised climax
of braking is all that any normal person
could expect. I have no visions of kinky
variations on the stiff, well-oiled chain.
Nor am I into make-up: let the instrument
be what it was designed for—riding quite
past the limits of pedestrian interest with a vigor.

Ed Orr

LEXICOGRAPHY

(A Trough of Low Pleasure)

Like a lepidopterist with a fine new specimen
Carried carefully home from a successful sortie,
What did I do with this marvellous trophy?
  Spread it out and put it under the microscope!

This, the *O.E.D.* in its Compact Edition,
Carried a reading glass, a standard extra.
What did I search for? Just like anyone,
  Looked up CUNT, to see it under the reading glass

(The same would have been done by the magazine editors
And by all the publishers, including Virago,
It's an important word and basic in folklore,
  Known about and spoken, over the hemispheres),

Keats's friends drank to it as Mater Omnium,
It's full of sexual overtones and sensual undertones,
It has a kind of inwardness that some call mystical.
  So I crept, so slowly, over the printed mass,

Not wanting to disturb it as it basked in the sunshine,
Tiptoeing in to net it. I reached CUNCTATION,
Which means delay, delaying, or tardy action;
  Turned the page, to CUNNING, under the reading glass.

I was sure I should see it, what a triumph! Quietly
I moved on to CUNSTER, a conner once in Scotland . . .
And then, in upper and lower case, I saw it:
  Cunt—: see CONT. Injustice! Under-represented!

When COCK is there in glory with words like CLAPPERDUD-
    GEON
(Meaning a man who was born and bred a beggar).
So I turned to CONT, in a mood of disappointment.
  It's "To punt (a boat, or barge)" over inland waterways!

PUNT for CUNT! That dictionary was joking!
Surely some scholar was laughing his head off!
I passed on, to the Supplement (CHIP-SPARROW, CLEAVAGE).
  Still not there! What sadness, under the microscope.

No wonderful butterfly opening wings and closing
Or even frozen timelessly in grave lexicography—
Absent without leave, as they said in my Army days!
  Shut the book and put it back, with the reading glass.

Gavin Ewart

5

LA VENGANZA DE LOS MUERTOS VIVIENTES

"Return to your villages.
We won't kill you any more."

—a Guatamalan general
quoted on the Evening News

The dead considered whether this promise
could be trusted. They did miss the life
of the village, the cheerful music blasting
from the loudspeaker in the square,
the bustle of the soldiers, the sense
of being part of a drama the whole world
was watching. But they'd grown confused
there in the mass grave, uncertain,
shy. And if they did return,
what could they do, being dead?
Spy on surviving relatives? Live like lizards
in the crevices of walls? *Quien sabe*,
maybe they should just stay planted
where they were, learning ecology.

But the general had summoned them—
they had no choice. They pushed their way up
through the teeming topsoil to emerge
into the Technicolor day, looking exactly
as you'd imagine. And not, of course, able
to repress the natural instinct
of corpses in this classic situation.
Even the withered *abuelita*—"Granny" to us
gringoes—must gnaw at the young corporal's
shinbone; such is the law of retribution.
So what can we do, up here in the north,
to mend matters? I've no idea—
but the President has suggested we send
arms and advisors to help stop the killing.

Tom Disch

124•

AWARDS

I

A gold medal to the inventor of the bed,
cozier than cars, less sandy than beaches.

Gold too to the genius
who invented the bathroom,
arena of the washing and fondling of the nether regions
with the ooze and stink of the forbidden,
and the miraculous flushing away.

And a medal for inventing coffee and the cigarette
that, shared, bring heads together over table tops,
making conversation intimate,
and perhaps join hands under it.
O for another lifetime to atone
for having to stop smoking in this one.

A special award for lunch, senseless but divine
eating in early afternoon,
especially things like hotdogs that are fun
to munch on walking in the sun—
I feel right now like having one.
And a string of prizes certainly should
go to the brilliant inventor of food.

For clothes and its many useless pieces,
shirts with buttonholes, belts, and ties,
pleated skirts and pants with creases,
the inventor deserves a booby prize:
What a time to get them on, those complicated shapes,
instead of simple wrap-arounds and drapes.

Another booby prize to the inventor
of mankind's worst tormentor, sex—
and really let's confess, it hardly every works.
I'm thinking not only of the sticky mess
but the urological complications, pregnancy, VD—

though I'd award a special medal for
the divinest of all inventions maybe,
the consolation prize for sex's failure:
the human baby.

But to the inventor of romance, that world of illusion
in novel, opera, and soap opera enshrined,
the biggest booby prize:
It only exists in the adolescent mind
and it's all lies.

II

The Medal of the Empire to the conductors collecting fares
on those miraculously-unbattered red double-decker buses—
for running up and down the curving stairs,
calling you luv and ducky as they manipulate
levers on the machine for making change,
and cranking another gadget yoked around their necks,
spin out ticker tapes of tickets,
and all without becoming nervous wrecks—
it's not their fault it costs a fortune for a ride.

In fact, the English working class should get a prize
for putting up with the crap they take
and giving back their luv and ducky
with such kind and cheerful eyes.

They're obviously a whole other people from the lords,
those invaders from abroad who pushed them to the bot-
        tom.
Island dwellers, they felt safe with their surrounding sea
and danced around the maypole thoughtlessly
until waves of conquering teutonic hordes
herded them off to mine and mill
where they go on working for a pittance
in the legendary damp and chill,
when there are jobs at all, that is . . . O innocence . . .
It's a complete mystery to me
why they support the royals in luxury

when they could pack them off to Estoril.
But no, they dutifully offer up their asses
to the upper classes
who keep them firmly in their place.

How soulful they are, how dear,
and though it's not something they'd like to hear,
almost like an Arab race.

Edward Field

LUNCH AT THE STANDISH HOTEL

Lady Wellington was giggish,
Lady Chatterton was priggish,
Lady Bellingham was smallish,
Lady Featherly was biggish,
As they munched at the Standish
Where the prices were outlandish.

Lady Wellington had a sniffle,
Lady Chatterton ate a waffle,
Lady Bellingham loved to gossip,
Lady Featherly said, "How awful,"
As they lunched at the Standish
Where the prices were outlandish.

Lady Wellington wore the latest fashions,
Lady Chatterton deplored politicians,
Lady Bellingham deplored Lady Chatterton,
Lady Featherly collected for a Mission,
As they lunched at the Standish
Where the prices were outlandish.

Lady Wellington was clever,
Lady Chatterton had a cleaver
& beheaded Lady Bellingham,
Lady Featherly cried, "Well, I never!"
As they lunched at the Standish
Where the prices were outlandish.

Lady Wellington quite fainted,
Lady Chatterton repented,
Lady Bellingham was buried,
Lady Featherly relented,
As they lunched at the Standish
Where the prices were outlandish.

Louis Phillips

ME WEE BOGGY DOON

When wee boggy doon
grumps o'er me,
to screech the sinew
of me mushroom brain,
and sops the starch
from rickety mind
and frazzle-frame,
and methinks mefeels
me toady dingle shrink—

then me ghosts away
to thistles and the pipes,
abandons scare for
Highland's special showetry;
and joins wee raucous spirits
shrewdish in such knowetry,
to expunge me guts of this
Edgar Allan Poetry.

So we gimbles and gyres
in the ghastly wabe,
and rasps and slithers to
the pipes of Murdoch's Fling;
and raises in praise
Wee Bobbie's bleeding bones
(and other carefully-selected
Scotty poems), as we shun
the dewy dank of boggy doon!

Aye, we stags this eve
will have our fill,
where glints gay moon
upon MacGregor's holy still;
to nibble on the moldy fern,
a side of venison; consume
a gang of Burns and reconsider
some of Tennyson;

to buck the drought of
writer's scaley blight,
by chasing dark to
lacey, dew-decked dawn;
to skitter-scamper with
the elve and fawn,
'til finally 'tis
'bye, 'bye,
me boggy doon!

Russ Traunstein

KALISPERA

On Crete one night at the Palace Theatre,
anti-climax to more authentic ruins,
I saw a Bondish movie with Mycénean titles
in which the lovely Hellene spy, after fruitless

encounters with the agent, finally offers
herself (flash/flesh) like a bowl of muscats.
Whereupon out of the winedark audience
on holiday from marble breasts,
a native goatboy spouts a Dionysian "Ha-ha?"
laughing all the way out of the Minoan columns,
all the way down the agora,
pan into the topless evening, the kalispera.

What laughter! What discovery!
What scorn for the censors who'd only allowed
a grape-fly peep at cinéflesh!
At first his ha-has stung the air
like gouts from the interrogative Aegean.
Then they settled down and sailed,
gulls on the updraft, crying epithets,
crying Malista! Endaksi! Paracaló!
Please—show loveliness as it is!
Evcharisto! Thanks for naked skies!

A. L. Lazarus

COSMOPOLITAN JUMP ROPE SONG

Sally Sally Arteseros
Took a shopping trip to Paris:
Dior
    Hermés
        Houbigant
Rojas
    Ricci
        Saint Laurent
Worth
    Givenchy
        Revillon
Chanel
    Balmain
        Guerlain
            Grés
Lanvin
    Lancôme
        Mainbocher
Caron
    Carven
        Cartier
Champagne
    Chablis
        Beaujolais
Vouvray
    Cognac
        Grand Marnier
Camembert
    Roquefort
        Port Salut
Pont l'Evêque
    Brie
        Et Bleu

●131

Paté
    Foie Gras
        Quiche
            Fondu
Mornay
    Beurre Blanc
        Béarnaise
Veau
    Tournedos
        Bouillabaise
Crêpes Suzette
    Mousse
        Soufflé
Parfait
    Marrons
        Crême Brulée.
She put them in a paper sack,
Took a plane and brought them back.
In all the land now who's the fairest?
Sally Sally Arteseros.

Pyke Johnson, Jr.

AN ITALIAN GARDEN

(After an article in the *New York Times*, 9/11/80, "Gardening Italian Style")

If you clip your hedge and set out a concrete
birdbath, you are gardening like an Italian.

If you shape your shrubs geometrically
and keep lead ornaments about, you are approaching
the full Italian taste.

If you employ brick walks, wooden gates,
and have a well-clipped lawn, you are gardening

in the Italian style as reflected
through the gardens of Victorian and Edwardian England.

If you erect masonry terraces,
marble flights of stairs, arcades, you are gardening
(and engineering as well) in the Italian
style as reflected through the gardens of
Victorian and Edwardian England via Hollywood.

If you surround your property with topiary sculpture—
lions and tigers and bears, ho! ho!—you are gardening
most fancifully in the Italian style
as reflected through the gardens of Victorian etc.
via Hollywood according to *The Wizard of Oz.*

If you long for a statue of Byron
encircled by a fine yew hedge, if you cherish
gracefully designed concrete tubs
that hold simple annuals, if you have ever used
a cast-iron lamp standard in the shape
of a Doric column or the classic
urn of a table lamp set on a homemade plinth,
painting them to resemble French terra cotta, I would guess,
however well or badly life has treated you,
you have a real nice Italian garden.

Jane Flanders

PIPPA PASSES,
BUT I CAN'T GET AROUND THIS TRUCK

Morning's at seven,
The plane's at the airport
God's in his Heaven,
But I'm still in Fairport.

Margaret Blaker

GEOGRAPHY LESSON
or A GRAMMARIAN'S FUNERAL

North is *up*,
  Which should be plain,
And East is *back*
  Except for Maine.
It's *Down* East,
  Down South the same,
While West is *out*
  To end the game.
We hold these prepositions to be self-evident.

Pyke Johnson, Jr.

EPITAPH

I was born in Missouri.
I died in Nevada.
What happened in between
Didn't much matter.

James Preston

GETTING OFF IN CHICAGO

Where are you?
  Chicago.
Where about?
  How do I know,
this telephone booth
only the second place I been
beside the bus station.

Look outside
read a street sign.
  Okay.
What it say?
  Say
WALK, DONT WALK.

Wallace Whatley

BEHIND AN RV

Being stuck behind an RV
is like seeing your life
pass before your eyes.

You can't pass on the left,
and you can't pass on the right,
so you begin to notice

things, like the names of sidestreets:
Glen Cove and Lost River, you think
one of these will appeal to the RV

but they don't. Cars are piling
up so you notice the trees,
how green they are

with subtle variations in shade,
light green, middle green, and dark green
and you wonder if the RV sees

this, whether there are Hostess cupcakes
in the kitchen, and whether
there is room to turn around

and you go back to your childhood,
still thirty miles an hour
in a fifty mile zone

and you remember what camping
was then, just a pup tent
and usually in the back yard.

Judith Skillman

BLUE CARIBOU

They were harnessed to a silver hearse.
She supposed them to be a mirage.
Henry was particular by nature—
the carburetor wouldn't start.
The inn, however, was charming,
their suite done up in peach
matching the ribbons on her nightie.
Touches like that helped.

Jean Balderston

BALLADE OF THE BRIGHT ANGEL*

"O happy horse, to bear the weight of Antony!"

(A&C, I,v,21)

Stuffed into denim, grinning in Polaroid,
Sneakers and shoulder bags banging, they lurch and sway
Through Paleozoic sandstone, overjoyed
To be out of their cars at last and chafing their way
Down the ages of the Grand Canyon; and every day
Their mounts inherit new human crosses to carry.
Only the guide and his choice are joined to stay.
O happy mule, to bear the weight of Jerry!

Neck-stroking co-eds, machos loudly annoyed
To be stuck near the rear, matrons who must weigh
More than the chuck box, snake phobics even Freud
Would toss from the couch, equestrians hot to display
Inappropriate talents, students of Zane Grey
Who holler whoa! and giyyup! in accents that vary
From Youngstown to Stockholm to Dallas to Mandalay—
O happy mule, to bear the weight of Jerry!

Kicking their captive steeds along the void,
Pummeling soft ears with a ceaseless bray
Of past excursions, pizza, paranoid
State troopers, ƒ stops, prices in Santa Fe
And the world's most adorable grandchildren, are they
En route to Phantom Ranch or Canterbury?
Who cares, with apple cores for overpay?
O happy mule, to bear the weight of Jerry!

The Bright Angel Trail, the most popular route down the Grand Canyon; the Fred Harvey Co., the mule-trip concessionaire; and Phantom Ranch, the trail's destination on the Colorado River.

Fred Harvey, it's a tacky crowd today.
O happy hand, to team up with the very
Jewel of your help that runs on hay.
And happy Jewel, to bear the weight of Jerry!

Bruce Berger

EVENING ROUND-UP

The city gal
Has lots of fun
Spending her days
In dude-ranch sun,
But dusk brings dates
With guys in jeans
Who soon make clear
What "ranch hand" means.

Dick Hayman

MOMENT OF TRUTH

I'm glad I'm not beautiful;
The beautiful are always being molested.
I'm glad I'm not wealthy;
The wealthy are always being robbed.
I'm glad I'm not powerful;
The powerful are always being assassinated.
I'm glad I'm not famous;
The famous are always being mobbed.
I'm glad I'm just what I am;
An average, ordinary, everyday
Liar!

Loralee Meighen

SOME GOOD SHIT

No officer,
how fast
was I going?

8.

Hal J. Daniel III

YOUNG THOMAS'S DREAM

Homage to Thomas Hood

Young Thomas was a handsome youth
  Whose features were serene.
His hair was dark, his heart was light,
  His neck was in between.

In college Tom applied his wits,
    B.A. and M.A. earning,
And by degrees crept up back stairs
    Toward high front tiers of learning.

Yet Thomas nightly tossed and turned.
    Bad dreams made Thomas weep.
Nightmares singled Thomas out
    And coupled in his sleep.

He dreamt he turned a thief and stole
    From school at wintertime,
Forsaking academic halls
    To seek the hauls of crime.

He dreamt he tampered with the mails,
    Was caught, and put in fetters.
Police gave him the third degree
    For turning Doctor of Letters.

But Tom would not confess his guilt
    And so went up for trial.
When pressed his misdeeds to affirm,
    He made a firm denial.

Poor Tom's attorney turned up drunk
    And unsure of his basis.
He'd practiced at the bar too long
    And had too many cases.

The prosecuting lawyer, though,
    Was sober, Scotch, and wry.
He understood the jury sat
    To give young Tom the lie.

The jury when they heard his speech
    Were spellbound. No one napped.
They'd all been put into a box,
    Addressed, and now were rapt.

The jury brought the verdict in:
  "Guilty passing doubt."
The Judge gave sentence then, and it
  Was straightway carried out.

"Young Thomas," said the Judge, "by Fate
  Your needle has been threaded.
Your hopes have been defeated, and
  Now you must be beheaded."

"A-lack! a-lack!" young Thomas cried,
  "How all my prospects scoff!
I thought to tread the straight and narrow,
  And *not* to be headed *off*."

"Your fate is read," the Judge replied,
  "But don't be feeling blue;
A lad till lately very winsome
  Must look to lose some too."

"But the judgment is extreme," Tom wailed,
  And then expatiated:
"My life shall shortly be curtailed
  When I'm decapitated."

He wiped a tear from either eye,
  Then bowed before the court.
"I'll speak no longer now," he said,
  "Since I should be cut short."

The headsman was no gay young blade;
  A heavy axe he swung;
His face was grim, and he had played
  With blocks when he was young.

He raised his axe with motion slow.
  Young Thomas shook with dread.
Then fear succumbed to panic, so
  Of course, he lost his head.

The sun rose up the morrow morn,
    The clouds with rose adorning.
Young Thomas woke, and sighed to see
    The earth in robes of morning.

Then gingerly he felt his neck.
    Although his dream was past,
He could not think that he was quick
    Unless his head were fast.

Young Thomas, wholesome, happy lad,
    Displayed a golden mien.
His voice was soft, his vest was loud,
    But his neck *still* in between.

Laurence Perrine

SUBURBAN KILLER DAVE DUDLEY DECIDES HE WON'T CONFESS AFTER ALL

After he sawed off the baby's head
stabbed the dog
and dragged the wife's entrails
two times around the shrubs
he heard a droning
overhead.

Tourists squinted out jet windows
during take-off.
There the bump and shove of traffic,
there the ballpark cute as a pin
and there the wedding-cake husband
watering his roses.

Michael Finley

6

POETS OBSERVED

Young poets swim in schools like minnows.
As time or tide their number winnows
A few survive in deeps, very
Wily, large, and solitary.

F. C. Rosenberger

A POLICEMAN'S LOT

"The progress of any writer is marked by those moments when he manages to outwit his own inner police system."

—Ted Hughes

Oh, once I was a policeman young and merry
                  (young and merry)
Controlling crowds and fighting petty crime
                  (petty crime)
But now I work on matters literary
                  (litererry)
And I am growing old before my time
                  ('fore my time).
No, the imagination of a writer
                  (of a writer)
Is not the sort of beat a chap would choose
                  (chap would choose)
And they've assigned me a prolific blighter
                  ('lific blighter)—
I'm patrolling the unconscious of Ted Hughes.

It's not the sort of beat a chap would choose
                  (chap would choose)—
Patrolling the unconscious of Ted Hughes.

All our leave was cancelled in the lambing season
                  (lambing season)
When bitter winter froze the drinking trough
                  (drinking trough)
For our commander stated, with good reason
                  (with good reason)
That that's the kind of thing that starts him off
                  (starts him off).
But anything with four legs causes trouble
                  (causes trouble)—
It's worse than organizing several zoos
                  (several zoos),

Not to mention mythic creatures in the rubble
                                   (in the rubble)
Patrolling the unconscious of Ted Hughes.

It's worse than organizing several zoos
                                   (several zoos)
Patrolling the unconscious of Ted Hughes.

Although it's disagreeable and stressful
                              (bull and stressful)
Attempting to avert poetic thought
                                ('etic thought),
I could boast of times when I have been successful
                                 (been successful)
And conspiring compound epithets were caught
                              ('thets were caught).
But the poetry statistics in this sector
                                  (in this sector)
Are enough to make a copper turn to booze
                                  (turn to booze)
And I do not think I'll make it to inspector
                                   (to inspector)
Patrolling the unconscious of Ted Hughes.

It's enough to make a copper turn to booze
                               (turn to booze)—
Patrolling the unconscious of Ted Hughes.

after W. S. Gilbert

Wendy Cope

ALL POETS' WIVES HAVE ROTTEN LIVES

All poets' wives have rotten lives,
Their husbands look at them like knives

(Poor Gertrude! poor Eileen!*
Nevermore seventeen!)
Exactitude their livelihood
And rhyme their only gratitude,
Knife-throwers all, in vaudeville,
They use their wives to prove their will.

Delmore Schwartz (1943)

Gertrude Buckman, the first Mrs. Delmore Schwartz. Eileen B. Mulligan, the first Mrs. John Berryman.

"CAME AWAY WITH BETJEMAN TO PULL HIM ALONG THROUGH WULFSTAN UNTIL DINNER TIME"

C. S. Lewis' Diary (1927)*

Come away, Betjeman! Pull for the shore!
Pull on through Wulfstan and anglo that sax!
This is the tune that entices us more
Than vernal Vaughan-Williams or beautiful Bax!
We can be happy, so happy, we twain,
With liege-lord and serf and intransigent thane!

Come away, Betjeman! Mince down the High,
Think not of Wystan or sorbets or sex!
Drink not the wine, of the neatherd's young thigh
All the enchantment can only perplex!
Plain living, high thinking—of such there's a dearth,
We'll raise it and praise it on our Middle Earth!

Gavin Ewart

At Oxford University in 1927 C. S. Lewis was John Betjeman's Tutor. Lewis regarded him as a hopeless young aesthete, and indeed Lewis' attempts to interest him in Anglo-Saxon all ended in failure.

THE BLUE PLATE TEA ROOM: SESTINA

When Robert Frost came barding down to Hartford,
Some middle meddler rang up Wallace Stevens
To meet for lunch at some "place called The Blue Plate
Tea Room, because there was no other place,"
Wrote Stevens.* In October '42
You let things roll the way they had to roll.

They couldn't welcome Frost with fife and drum roll.
And as for what they'd eat in wartime Hartford,—
Butter was rationed, back in '42
(You wouldn't know it, though, to look at Stevens,
Or Frost)—I'd guess, at that time, in that place,
Both of them muttered, "Well. I'll take the Blue Plate

Special" (which must have been served *on* a blue plate,
One pitty-pat of margarine per roll).
The waitress slung them down each in their place.
"How do you do it, Wally, here in Hartford?"
Frost would have chaffed him, looking hard at Stevens,
And laughed a laugh pure 1942.

We still make movies set in '42.
Their soundtracks catch the clatter of The Blue Plate
But so far haven't dubbed the words of Stevens,
Which could have been, "*Ça va.* The barrel roll
Is not attempted often now in Hartford.
What do you say we drive past Clemens' place?"

Their conversation's one you can't quite place,
Stamped with the dateline 1942.
TWO POETS MEET AND EAT, the Daily Hartford
Times could have had it: "In the modest Blue Plate
Tea Room, two men securely on the roll
Of poets, Robert Frost and Wallace Stevens . . ."

*Letters of Wallace Stevens, p. 423.

Later, as afternoon rolled under, Stevens
Wrote Frost he hoped that some time out at his place
(Asylum Avenue) they'd eat an eggroll
Of Blue Plate language, saved from '42,
And say goodbye just like they'd left The Blue Plate,
Shaking big hands in Anglo-Saxon Hartford.

Envoy: The Shooting Script

SCENE: Hartford. CU SHOT OF Wallace Stevens
Inside The Blue Plate Tea Room—dumpy place.
OUTSIDE: a '42 Ford. Frost steps down. *ROLL 'EM!*

John Ridland

NOTES ON WRITERS: THREE CLERIHEWS

Handsome John Keats
performed many feats.
None of higher order
than writing on water.

*

William Makepeace Thackeray
never drank a daiquiri.
But with hot enchiladas
he'd quaff piña colladas.

*

Wystan Auden would often appear
with companions not quite *de rigueur.*
"My dear, I know they're losers;
but buggers can't be choosers."

Robert Phillips

TO WORDSWORTH

O see the happy daffodils
Now nodding in the rain.
I wish to God I knew some way
To cause the [   ] pain.*

*The text of the final verse is corrupt. We agree with Ezra Pound who agrees with Dr. Ker who
rejects "charmers" as without foundation in the MS tradition.

F. F. Burch

ESSAY ON ENJAMBMENT

Once clauses in poems weren't quartered and chopped;
At the ultimate pauses a reader's voice dropped,
Which was why such lines were called end-stopped.
But then assorted poets like Shakespeare started
To ignore line endings. Verbs and their objects parted
Company to face life divided and broken-hearted.
Now free versify-
ing is even deny-
ing the sacred unify-
ing bonds of words by pry-
ing them apart and si-
phoning end-stop off with endless hy-
phening. And going one b-
etter, poetic go-g-
etters are releasing l-
etters from traditional f-
etters. V-
Vhere, my friends, v-
vill this lust to lop
end? Stop!

Raymond Griffith

FOUR EPIGRAMS

On a Poet

He sought in his late work, which no one reads,
The unavailing laurel of the Swedes.

On a Teacher

Chinless and slouched, gray-faced and slack of jaw,
Here plods depressed Professor Peckinpaugh,
Whose work J. Donald Adams found "exciting."
This fitted him to teach Creative Writing.

On a Philosopher

The world is everything that is the case.
Now stop your blubbering and wash your face.

On a Scholar

Ascribed to earth, by bookworms tilled and ploughed,
She wore her learning lightly, like a shroud.

Donald Hall

MAKING IT

He picks up a table knife
large as a machete and sharp enough
to cut an overdone potato
or warm ice cream.
He hacks off a chunk of butter,
spreads it everywhere: on the Narragansett
oyster fleet, joggers in rut, a large frame
house on Main Street, someone's random
family, a shortstop, his thumb.

The world is my toast he cries
and slaps a load on the Civil War.
A few people notice their ability
to move their arms and legs
has become more ponderous, studied,
and the general pavement slicker
than they remember. *Don't worry*
he says to them. *You are the special ones*
I have chosen to devote the rest of my life to.
He goes down on his knees before them
and begins to lick them clean.

Dabney Stuart

MY CONFESSIONAL SESTINA

Let me confess. I'm sick of these sestinas
written by youngsters in poetry workshops
for the delectation of their fellow students,
and then published in little magazines
that no one reads, not even the contributors
who at least in this omission show some taste.

Is this merely a matter of personal taste?
I don't think so. Most sestinas
are such dull affairs. Just ask the contributors
the last time they finished one outside of a workshop,
even the poignant one on herpes in that new little magazine
edited by their most brilliant fellow student.

Let's be honest. It has become a form for students,
an exercise to build technique rather than taste
and the official entry blank into the little magazines—
because despite its reputation, a passable sestina
isn't very hard to write, even for kids in workshops
who care less about being poets than contributors.

Granted nowadays everyone is a contributor.
My barber is currently a student
in a rigorous correspondence school workshop.
At lesson six he can already taste
success having just placed his own sestina
in a national tonsorial magazine.

Who really cares about most little magazines?
Eventually not even their own contributors
who having published a few preliminary sestinas
send their work East to prove they're no longer students.
They need to be recognized as the new arbiters of taste
so they can teach their own graduate workshops.

Where will it end? This grim cycle of workshops
churning out poems for little magazines
no one honestly finds to their taste?
This ever-lengthening column of contributors
scavenging the land for more students
teaching them to write their boot camp sestinas?

Perhaps there is an afterlife where all contributors
have two workshops, a tasteful little magazine, and sexy
        students
who worshipfully memorize their every sestina.

Dana Gioia

A POET DEFENDED

You claim his poems are garbage. Balderdash!
Garbage includes some meat. His poems are trash.

Paul Ramsey

WEARY FROM READING CERTAIN COMPETENT POETS MY DOG AND I GO FOR A WALK IN THE CEMETERY

The small grey grocers
scurry through the aisles
busy among the buckeyes
acorns beechnuts busy
busy busy
among the twigs and leaves.

No busier than Bosch
who runs them
down the rows of stones
and up a tree.

Peter Klappert

YOUNG POET'S LAMENT

To be charming in a world that's lost its charm,
To be delighted in a world that's lost delight
      I might
Speak about the freckles on her arm,
Her sweet face blushing in the morning light.

But other poets did that, did that well.
For other mistresses they pined and sighed
      And tried
By every stratagem they knew to cast a spell
To turn them into creatures they could ride.

She didn't need such words. Almost
Before I could pronounce her name
            She came
Against me in my bed and tossed
The blankets back, embraced me without shame.

What then of mystery? How can
I practice praising when the one I'd praise
            Has raised
Her body to my own, has spoiled my plan
To woo her slowly and to leave her dazed?

Yet speak, she tells me, speak of soul and heart.
Tell me what they said, those silly men.
            And then
If love and lust prove somehow worlds apart
Slow down Time. Have at me with your pen.

Dick Allen

A CAT'S PURR

The nice thing about a cat's purr
is knowing your cat is happy
and taking credit for it.
Wives and children don't work that way.

The nice thing about a cat's purr
is knowing your cat is happy.
But I had to dump Angela off my lap
to write this down.

Not one to harbor a grudge,
she's at it again.
I also admire
her tail.

Knute Skinner

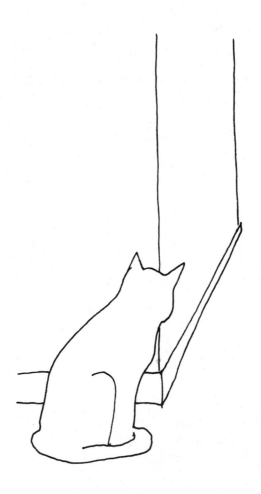

BOOTING UP

You touch my reset button, making
my screen go wavy, and then blank.
My disc-drives groan. My system checks
and loads. Then I have you to thank

for software lighting up my hardware
and rippling signals through my CRT.
My ROM begins to tingle when your RAM
absorbs the data from each input key,

filling our memories with kilobytes
of information processed, indexed, stored
in streams of on and off which bring to life
inert connections on our circuit board.

Oh, never shall my drive refuse to log
so long as chips have juice—and you to boot.
Come slip into this port: my CPU,
without your floppy disc, cannot compute.

Judson Jerome

DEAR WRITER

In reply to your recent inquiry,
we have lost your poems.

If we had not,
we would undoubtedly have said unkind things;
therefore we consider
we have done you a favor.

Should you have others,
we wish you better luck
in placing them elsewhere.

Sincerely, The Editors

P.S. Enclosed please find the revised guidelines
for renewing your subscription.

Bruce Bennett

IF I HAD BEEN CALLED SABRINA OR ANN, SHE SAID

I'm the only poet with the name.
Can you imagine a prima ballerina named
Marge? Marge Curie, Nobel prize winner.
Empress Marge. Fat chance. My lady
Marge? Never. Marge/large/barge/
charge. It is, in its essence, humorous.
In literature applied to giggling adolescents,
waitresses. Definitely working class.
Any attempt to doll it up
(Mar-gee? Mar-gette? Margelina?
Margarine?) makes it worse. Name
like an oil can, like a bedroom
slipper, like a box of baking soda,
useful, plain; impossible for foreigners,
from French to Japanese, to pronounce.
My own grandmother called me what
could only be rendered in English
as Mousie. O my parents, what
you did unto me, forever. Even
my tombstone will look like a cartoon.

Marge Piercy

MISSING OUT

Like the philosopher says
I'm a bundle of perceptions.
Walking to my mailbox,
I perceive
I'm missing out.
No famous novelists
Scribble me advice,
No well-known poet
Lectures me on craft,
Difficulties of free verse,
Necessity of Ekphrasis
& the 13 syllable line.
No hot gossip here
On angels, agents, & wives,
The literary life etc.
Somebody about to be divorced
& reviewed in that order.
No spilling the beans
On the latest plot,
No latent symbols
Climbing out of the closet,
No authenticated signatures
So when I'm down & out
I can run to an auctioneer
With numinous sacred texts.
Oh no. No exotic cachets,
Nothing written in cadence,
Just the usual bills,
A computerized threat,
One post card from Berkeley
Showing *The Princess and the Pea*,
One country store catalogue
That is certain to get read.

When I leave,
2 Chipmunks return.
They make their home in my mailbox.
They hate it when I get mail.

Louis Phillips

HOW THE GREAT POEM ELUDED THEM

"If you can't be an athlete, be an athletic supporter!"
With a line like that, how could any movie fail?
It's like watching a coach whose team resembles
the Keystone Cops, or the Three Stooges trying to build a
      house—
the coach keeps saying, "Get tough" or "Set up"
or "Let's play defense," and the crowd marvels
at his understanding of the game and feel for the players.
I don't know how much truth there is to this, but an in-
      formed
source said Houdini had to drop his most difficult
trick from the act, a feat which consisted of escaping
from a wet sheet, because it looked too simple.

Ed Orr

ON THE ECONOMICS OF PUBLISHING POETRY

The printer and the men who made
The paper and the ink were paid.
In our advanced economy
Only the verse is free.

F. C. Rosenberger

INTERTEXTUALITY

*In place of a hermeneutics
we need an erotics of art.*

—Susan Sontag

—I am a thing in a dustjacket trying
To make you read. Your eyes are soft and small
And want to scan an old text not at all.
They long to look at real men, standing, lying . . .
But twig yon volumes of back issues dying
In the remaindered pallor of the moon;
For I must feel the touch of such eyes soon.
I am a thing in a dustjacket trying.

—I am a ms. brand-new in beauty waiting
Until some young stud comes, and I do too.
But what grey tome among the stacks are you
Whose tones are dry as grass upon the lawn?
Out of my lap, you bore, before I yawn!
I am a ms. brand-new in beauty waiting.

William Harmon

TYPICAL OPTICAL

In the days of my youth
   'Mid many a caper
I drew with my nose
   A mere inch from the paper;
But now that I'm older
   And life has grown hard
I find I can't focus
   Inside of a yard.

First pill-bottle labels
   And telephone books
Began to go under
   To my dirty looks;
Then want-ads and box scores
   Succumbed to the plague
Of the bafflingly quite
   Unresolvably vague.

Now novels and poems
   By Proust and John Donne
Recede from my ken in
   Their eight-point Grandjon;
Long, long in the lens
   My old eyeballs enfold
No print any finer
   Than sans-serif **bold**.

John Updike

TAKE A LIBRARIAN TO LUNCH

Take a Librarian to lunch.
You know that she deserves it.
Ascertain her favorite food,
Then find a place that serves it.

Seek out, too, an ambience
That you are sure will suit her:
Some place that bans all little kids
And where there's no computer.

Serve her with her favorite drink:
Champagne? Or something diet?
And make it clear that, at this meal,
There are no rules on quiet.

Ask her to tell you of her job:
Which books are circulating?
Which patron said what funny thing?
You'll find it fascinating.

But do leave promptly when you've shared
Good talk and drink and food.
Librarians must be back when due,
And may not be renewed.*

Pyke Johnson, Jr.

*N.B. Nothing here should be construed as precluding the taking of a male Librarian to lunch.

FIX

I have been trying to place or fasten this word securely,
put it into a stable or unalterable form,
get a line upon it, as upon the position of a ship or aircraft,
to make of this word a substance nonvolatile or solid.

But it is difficult to direct the gaze (for example), steadily,
    to concentrate;
I find myself in a difficult or embarrassing position, a tight
    place,
as if through an instance of bribery or collusion
to prearrange the outcome (of a contest) by unlawful means.

I cannot establish definitely, specify, a time, a place,
or make a color, a drawing, a photographic image fast or
    permanent,
fasten an imputation or responsibility upon a person,
or ascribe or allot the blame.

It is no consequence of an intravenous injection of heroin,
nor of an attempt to spay or castrate an animal;
I do not need to take revenge upon, get even with, to kill
    or keep,
only to convert an object or situation to its proper state.

I am only trying to make ready, put together, prepare
the means to rectify, adjust, to restore, set right, repair,
to make a substance nonvolatile or solid,
to place or fasten this word securely in a stable or unalter-
    able form.

David Evett

PETER EXPLAINS WHY THE STUDENT LITERARY MAGAZINE DIDN'T COME OUT

Last spring I was having this
really strange relationship
with a girl who was dying
and heavily into sex.

I'll have more time
this semester.

Clemewell Young

STUDENT RATES

Semesters leave their clutter on the walls
Curling records of occasions missed
Used surfboards, bikes and waterbeds
Bargain weekends in the Virgin Isles
Mixers, lectures, concerts . . .
"TIME & LIFE AT STUDENT RATES."

F.F. Burch

A HIGH IQ IS OVERRATED BULL

I, even while I read the door's **PUSH**, pull.

William Harmon

A NOVEL CRIME

Though it looked like the perfect crime
it was only a matter of time;
for, eluding his fate
through page two ninety-eight,
he's been caught on page two ninety-nine.

Anthony D. Accampo

NOT SCREWING

Which is hardest to comprehend?
We know that in every story
either the characters do or
they don't, and of course if they do

we don't ask why. (We're not fools.)
But what if he doesn't screw her?
Now there's a story to worry
over and read right to the end.

David Huddle

from NEW IMPROVED COYOTE

Coyote filled his mouth
with pingpong balls and
paid Fox a visit.
"Murfle moomph," said Coyote.
"Ah yes," said Fox.
"I see your point."
And he filled his
mouth with lit cherry bombs.
"Boom," said Fox.
Coyote could see Fox's
point too, but he couldn't
say anything that pointed
because his mouth
was full of pingpong balls.

*

Sometimes in early spring
when the tiny buds were
just forming on the trees,
Fox, Coyote, Crow and Badger

would sit out on the damp grass
next to the river and tell each
other tales. But the tales
had to be very short, for the
wet grass would soak through
their pants and make their
bottoms itch.
One day, at the end
of spring, Coyote said,
"We've created
SHORT STORY."
But the days were getting
longer and the grass was drying out.
That's when Daniel Defoe
and Samuel Richardson
stumbled into the little
group and asked if they might help.
"No," said Coyote, noticing
their dry pants. "Neither
of you has paid your dues."

Greg Keeler

7

BIRCHERS

When I see Birchers lean completely right
Across the line of logical discourse
I like to think they will fall over.
Often you must have seen them full of crap
And loaded down with imaginary
Threats to the Bill of Rights and ways to guard
The white man's burden. And after they have
Bored the pants off everyone in town just
Like Jehovah's Witnesses rampaging
Down Main Street—even then they don't subside.
But I was going to say when Truth broke in
With all her matter of fact about the Jehovah's
Witnesses, I should prefer to have them
Collapse under the force of their very own
Pea-brained arguments than from a right cross.
One could do worse than be a swinger of Birchers.

Alec Bond

J. EDGAR HOOVER'S FILE ON SUMAC

Steely under their fur,
They stand around factories, railroads.
Infiltrate our slums.

They turn red.

Bonnie Jacobson

FASCISM

When doing something it's
Nice to know what
You're doing but
It isn't absolutely
Necessary.

R Bartkowech

BIRDS OF A FEATHER

Of holidays and special days
November has its share—
Thanksgiving and Election Day
Are both located there.

Is it just coincidence,
Or can there be a reason,
That we select a president
When turkeys are in season?

Hannah Fox

CANDIDATE

"Image"
and "Charisma"
confused the voters' eyes,
till few could tell the Good from the
Bad Guise.

Gloria Maxson

ON POLITICS

If Joe McCarthy
Had been less swarthy,
Or the other one, Gene,
Had been less clean. . . .

Roy Blount Jr.

ON INDUSTRIALISM

The road to Hell is paved.

Paul Ramsey

HARRY MEEDER'S PAINT STORE

A long time ago, in Portland, Oregon,
I passed almost daily on my way downtown
A store called "Harry Meeder's Paint Store."

It was not called Rainbo Center.
It was not called Harry's Tints 'n Hues.
It was not called The Dot & Stripe Shop.
It was not called Handyman's Happy Hunting Ground.

It was not called Phantasmagoriana.
It was not called A Many Splendored Thing.
It was not called The Kaleidoscope Konnexion.
It was not called The Pied Peacock Plus.

It was not called Local Color.
It was not called Thick & Thin.
It was not called The Old Brush-off.
It was not called You Gotta Be Puttin' Us On.

It was not called The Three Little Pigments.
It was not called The Prismatic Peddlar.
It was not called Come All Ye Paints and Thinners.
It was not called The Mad Splatter and Friends Supply
        Outfit.
It was not called The Garden of Earthly Delights,
        Mediums & Darks.

Indeed, it was not even called Spectrum Shmectrum.

It was called "Harry Meeder's Paint Store."
The new freeway came through like a tsunami
And carried it away.

Peter Ridgway Jordan

NEAR THE PHILIP MORRIS WAREHOUSES IN DURHAM, CITY OF MEDICINE, AS THE PERFUME OF TOBACCO CURING PERMEATES THE SHIFTLESS AIR

O *Treasures of the Vatican,**
O bright gold leaf, O bullish art!

At the corner service station,
Virginia Slim, proprietor,
Carries a soft little coffin
In his pocket, over his heart.

Michael McFee

**Philip Morris was the corporate sponsor of the lavish touring exhibition.*

NOAH

Rats scurry from the doomed ship's hold.
Fleas vamoose when the cat grows cold.
From toothless gramp to youngest pup,
Nature knows when the jig is up.

When earth is fouled beyond reprieve,
Will Noah have the sense to leave?
Will he take them two by two,
And what about me and you
And you and you and you and you?

James Camp

WHAT CAME FIRST, THE CHICKEN OR THE TEASPOON?

my hens want to know
why i am pinching their eggs . . .

should i tell them
i'm eating their babies?

Terry Cuthbert

A CONVERSATION

What's your name?

What does it matter to you?

Because I have a ticket for you.

What kind of ticket?

Well, I can't tell you unless I know your name.

But how can my name have any bearing on the ticket?

Well, it could change with your name.

Are you crazy?

No, my name is Sam.

Then I'm crazy.

Oh, so that's your name. Well, the ticket I have is for you to appear at Bellevue at 3 P.M. sharp to have your head examined.

What for?

Didn't you say you're crazy?

But not that way.

What other way is there?

I don't want to be questioned like this as if I was guilty of something.

Being crazy is not being guilty of anything. It's something you can't help.

Well, I'm not crazy.

Then you were lying.

I was lying.

Then I have a different ticket for you.

What is it this time?

A ticket to come with me to the police station.

What for?

For lying.

Arrest me for lying?

Sure.

Are you a policeman?

No.

Then how can you arrest me?

Because you're interested.

Interested! I'm horrified.

Then that's another name you go by. This definitely
needs questioning by the police. You must be hiding
something. You must have stolen a watch.

I stole nothing but my patience with you. I've taken too
much.

This is a citizen's arrest. Come with me. You have
confessed to lying, hiding under a pseudonym and
stealing.

David Ignatow

IN FEE SIMPLE

Let the man who claims
Possession and control
Prove that claim against
Termite, worm, and mole.

C. M. Seidler

MATERNAL GRAFFITO

An emptied nest
will be blessedest.

Rochelle Distelheim

RAZOR CUTS AT MR. JIMMIE'S AND THE DECLINE OF MID-WESTERN WISDOM

Mr. Jimmie, who cuts my hair,
is no philosopher.

My dad's advantage, I guess,
to have known barbers, not stylists.

He also knew butchers,
bartenders and their nomenclatures

which made wisdom a less long climb
for him. I haven't the time

in my days of successive changes
with friends who become close strangers.

Jim Reed

THE RED COW IS DEAD

Isle of Wight (AP)—Sir Hanson Rowbotham's favorite Red Polled cow
is dead. Grazing in the lush pastures of the Wellow Farm, she was bitten
on the udder by an adder.

—The Herald Tribune

Toll the bell, fellow,
This is a sad day at Wellow:
Sir Hanson's cow is dead,
His red cow,
Bitten on the udder by an adder.

Spread the bad news! What is more sudden,
What sadder than udder stung by adder?
He's never been madder, Sir Hanson Rowbotham.

The Red Polled cow is dead.
The grass was lush at very last,
And the snake (a low sneak)
Passed, hissed,
Struck.

Now a shadow goes across the meadow,
Wellow lies fallow.
The red cow is dead, and the stories go round.
"Bit in the teat by a dog in a fit."
"A serpent took Sir Hanson's cow—
A terrible loss, a king's ransom."

A blight has hit Wight:
The lush grass, the forked lash, the quick gash
Of adder, torn bleeding udder,
The cow laid low,
The polled cow dead, the bell not yet tolled
(A sad day at Wellow),
Sir Hanson's cow,
Never again to freshen, never again
Bellow with passion—
A ruminant in death's covenant,
Smitten, bitten, gone.
Toll the bell, young fellow!

E. B. White

TO A WASP

You must have chortled
finding that tiny hole
in the kitchen screen. Right
into my cheese cake batter
you dived,
no chance to swim ashore,

no saving spoon,
the mixer whirring
your legs, wings, stinger,
churning you into such
delicious death.
Never mind the bright April day.
Did you not see
rising out of cumulus clouds
that fist aimed at both of us?

Janice Townley Moore

MOUSE

Just now I wasn't quick enough.
The cat caught me.
His tooth went through my eye.
He mashed me up.
I've lost my voice.
Also I smell.

As I fall out
a reporter from NEWSDAY
is waiting to interview me.
He asks How was it?
I say Terrible. He says
How do you feel now? I say
Like a pile of shit.
He writes it down.

Virginia R. Terris

BOWLING ALLEY

The best part of a bowling alley
is that nobody's dead.
No one is even thinking (about being dead)
—& that is the best part (of a bowling alley).

Brooke Horvath

ON COMING TO NOTHING

Old friends, nearing senility,
we sit, every last prospect dim,
and think: The world was wrong about me . . .
but at least it was right about him.

Richard Moore

FASTIDIOUS

Long prompt
and punctual,
she loathed the impish fate
that would in death denote her as
"the late."

Gloria Maxson

THE LAST OBIT

The funeral of Lorne H. Weeks
of Kensington on the Cove
was held on Sunday afternoon
January 2, 1986
at the Davidson Funeral Home.
The service was conducted
by the late Reverend J. R. Squires.
A solo "Beautiful Garden of Prayer,"
was sung by the late Mrs. Sande Clark.
The choir sang "In the Sweet Bye and Bye,"
to the organ of the late Mrs. Fern Causely.
Pallbearers were the late David Barglobe,
Brian Moss, Miller Weeks, and Doctor
High B. Tidesmon. Flowerbearers were
the late Carmen Woodside, Allen Weeks,
Grant McDonald, and Michael Mahem.
Interment was in the

Lolette Kuby

THE OUTING

Newton, Mass., April 20: Five women ranging in age from 80 to 96
drowned this afternoon when a driverless car rolled across a rest home
lawn and sank in Crystal Lake.

—*New York Times*

It was more like a dream than an ending,
the lawn chairs adrift on the grass,
the elm trees parting politely

so that ladies kept waiting might pass
before Bartlett returns from the pantry
where he's won some affection at last.

They enter the lake without Bartlett,
and settle down in the sand;
the windows are closed, except Bartlett's,
the handle comes off in the hand;
and Bartlett goes right on romancing,
knowing that they'll understand.

They sit as they sat as they waited
for Bartlett in fine livery
who's taking them all Sunday driving
and bringing them back for tea,
but Bartlett has conquered some virtue
and lingers inside wistfully.

And now though he's diving to find them,
and even holds open the door,
there is little to say of his sorrow
as he floats them each back to the shore
where the others have come to verandas
to see the five ladies once more.

Dan Masterson

BEING CHAMP

How do you bring it off, being Champ?
You get yourself a camel's hair coat,
John Garfield, and go to visit your mother
Who scrubs the lobbies of Savings & Loans
And you slip her 50 bucks which she tucks
In her décolletage ("Why thank you, son!")
And people passing will often wax droll:

"Hey Champ, attaway!" "How's it hangin', Champ?"
But if, nonetheless, you're down a bit low,
Unable to sleep or exult, you stroll
Through the late-at-night city at 2 a.m.
Bound for a swank condominium,
Up in the lift, down the winedark hall,
And when the door opens it's Barbara Stanwyck,
Cigarette smoke, black slink of a gown,
Great knowing eyes a-smoulder, saying:
"Champ, attaway . . . how's it hangin', Champ?"
And you say "Barbara . . ."
And walk on in.

Barry Spacks

OUR LADY OF THE BOA FEATHERS

Higgledy-piggledy,
Angela Lansbury
would sooner camp than vamp.
With brio she embarks

to play straight to the house—
histrionically
drawing more faggots to
her feet than Joan of Arc.

Robert Phillips

THE SWEET SINGER OF HARTFORD

Lydia Sigourney, the Sweet Singer of Hartford, was described by Henry James as "glossily ringletted and monumentally breastplated."

Higgledy-piggledy
Breastplated Lydia,
Glossily ringletted—
Sad her demise!—

Was in her poetry
Ultra-exhortative;
Said once at Bunker Hill:
"Monument, rise!"

William Jay Smith

LES FOLIES BERGÈRES: THE TWENTIES

Patty-cake Patty-cake
Mademoiselle Josephine
Baker, on finding Saint
Louis a bore,

Came out in Paris quite
Primitivistical—
Bunch of bananas was
All that she wore.

William Jay Smith

TEMPER TANTRUM IN A POETRY WORKSHOP

Dadaists, doodooists:
Abu M. Dakiki
counted his dactyls on
fingers and toes.

Dachshunds and dodos and
dactylological
dabblers in caca should
perfect their prose.

Peter Klappert

THE STARS COME OUT

Higgledy-piggledy,
Nicky Copernicus,
Ptolemy's rival for
Solar esteem,

Stumbling onto his
Heliocentrical
Paradigm, grumbled, "It's
Rather extreme!"

*

Jiminy Whillikers,
Corduroy, turtleneck
Mediastronomers
Sagan & Co.

Bring us the universe
News and the weather. De-
Lightful but also a
Little *de trop*.

J. Patrick Lewis

REMAINDERED TITLES AT BARNES & NOBLE

1. Arguments for the Existence of God

Last night on the way to a movie
I noticed that my watch had stopped.
Being already late, in all probability,
I was anxious to know the exact time,
And it wasn't possible along that stretch
Of Sixth Avenue to see the Met Life
Tower. So I tried to stop
Someone going the other direction,
But before I could say more than "Pardon me, sir,"
He gave me a nickel, and hurried on by.
"In God We Trust," a mint somewhere
Had stamped on the nickel. I reached
The movie just as the credits were starting,
And the next morning I bought another Timex.

2. History of the Theories of Rain

Every so often when the moon is full
I'll notice it, but not invariably. Or I'll encounter
Some peculiarly telling type of cloud and wonder
What to call it. Trees, flowers, birdsongs—
All languages I never learned. But I think
I can explain the rain. Put a low wide bowl
Of water atop the radiator (assuming
Its ribs allow this to be done): little by little
The water vanishes, drawn to the sky
By a scientific principle. In a few days
It will rain, if not here then in another city,
Blotting the moon from sight, making the mud
That feeds the trees and flowers, and earning money
For the men who sell umbrellas
From the doorways of bankrupt stores.

Tom Disch

ENTROPY

entropy does not concern mass man
but everyday
more & more socks are being lost

John Knoll

APATHY IN ACTION

Indifference vegetates
On flabby dispositions
With more inertia than momentum.
Lip service speaks up a hurricane
Without making waves
Or ripples,
Or as much as a breeze.
Like cold jello,
Comfortable in its bowl,
An anemic attitude
Only responds when shook.
Tomorrow, muscles will move
And the fat will shake,
No sweat.

Milt Hammerly

TELL GALILEO

Tell Galileo
to die.
Never recant.

No.
You tell him.

Phyllis Hotch

PIPEDREAM

It wasn't tucked
Away. Too bad.
The sign said DUCT
I wish I had.

Edmund Conti

IMPRECATED UPON A POSTAL CLERK

Nor rain nor snow nor heat nor gloom of night
Can stay this surly civil servant safe
Behind the counter from imposing his
Confusion, slothful rudeness and delay
Upon the simplest procedures of exchange.

May he bring his children up on Grade-B milk,
Continue less intelligent than lint,
Bid thirteen spades in No-Trump out of greed,
And have real trouble finding his own ass
With both hands and a mirror and a torch.

Howard Nemerov

SATISFACTION HAIKU

In high school he was the smart one,
starred in basketball, got all the girls.

Now look, he is balder than I am.

Eve Merriam

TRISTIA V, 8

Lowest of low, lower than lowest, you are immense,
   a phenomenon, man! I'd thought I had fallen as far
as a person could fall, to the very bottom of life's barrel.
   But under the barrel, look, there is a slug,
and underneath the slug, there is slimy nasty stuff,
   and there you are, underneath that. Amazing!
To mock someone like me, despite the fact that I suffer,
   or rather because I suffer—what kind of beast
wouldn't display compassion to a poor fellow creature
   in such distress? A mad dog will relent
when the animal it has attacked offers its throat, but you
   have no such limits. Fortune may yet teach you
a little of what you need to learn. The giddy goddess
   on her dizzying wheel delights in such reversals,
as Nemesis loves to bring down those whose arrogant
      pride
   invites her severe attention. People who laugh
at shipwrecks often drown, and the rest of us have to
      approve
   the justice of it. Those who mock at beggars
wind up sucking stones and feeling their bellies
   growl and grumble, exacting a cruel revenge.
You think it can't happen? I was once riding high;
   I had my day, but that kind of roll can't last
any more than a fire one makes of straw—it burns
   bright but quick, and then it's colder than ever.
There still could be another shuffle and deal, and I
   might come back. Caesar could change his mind
at any moment, bring me home, grant me a favor,
   whatever I want . . . And I shall remember you,
and make you the proper gesture of recompense for your
      long
   and unremitting hatred. Poetic justice?
I am a poet, remember, and sometimes we make
      suggestions
   that those with the real power find engaging.

But better than that, I'd rather simply stand and watch
   as you bring yourself down, which is more than likely.
Given the kind of hemorrhoidal ass-hole you are
   in your nasty heart, I'd bet a bundle on it.
I may even send a note expressing my deep regret
   that I can't be with you at such a trying time.

from The Tristia of Ovid,
translated by David R. Slavitt

A WISE QUESTION

Some Rockefeller said to me one day
(He saw me hide a poem inside my coat)
"If you're so smart, smar, why ain't you rich?"
What could I say to the son of a bitch?
"If you're so rich, why ain't you smart?"
(Had I but irony like Thomas Mann's,
I'd turn it on myself! If I were he
Before I'd be the President of Germany,
I'd turn it on myself, if I were he!

Delmore Schwartz (1942)

"LOOK, YOU CAN SEE THE ISLANDS FROM HERE!"

for Doug Johansen

At some point during the rescue
he became distracted. Perhaps it was
the lipsticked blonde poised upon the shore
in a gesture of uncompromising beauty.

192●

The deliberateness of his scissor kick
became sloppy, and as his grip
loosened over the coughing man's chest
their bodies reassumed the vertical.

Worst of all was the look
on the would-be-saved man's face
when for a moment their eyes met
in a fierce tread of water

reminiscent of virtue and the rescuer's
wife. Yet it took great courage
or vanity to swim away. For once he was not
too considerate to tell the truth.

Mark Irwin

MR. EXTINCTION, MEET MS. SURVIVAL

They're always whispering:
missing buttons, crow's-feet,
rust—
and I try to ignore them at first,
but they keep it up:
half-soles, dry rot,
biopsies, Studebakers—
that does it,
and I have to yell back:
virgin wool! fresh coffee! tennis balls!
new pennies! robins!
and that holds them awhile,
but they always come again,
sometimes at night, sometimes
in crowded elevators: *loose shingles,*
they whine, *soil erosion, migraines,*
dented fenders. I hold my ears

and shout: *high tide! fresh bread!*
new shoes! oranges! and people around me nod
and straighten their shoulders and smile,
and I think for a moment I've won—
but of course you never win,
and it gets to be almost a game:
they give me *oil spills,*
sewage sludge, tobacco smoke;
I come back with *swimming pools,*
butterflies, corn fields!
They give me *Calcutta,*
Gary, Coney Island;
I rattle off *Windermere,*
Isfahan, Bloomington—but
by the time I'm at work
it gets serious, all
lapsed memberships and *auto graveyards*
and *partial dentures* and *sub-*
committees and *leaves in the eaves,*
and right there at my desk I bellow:
daffodils! and *sailboats!* and *Burgundy!*
and *limestone!* and *birch trees!* and *robins,*
damn it, robins! and my boss
pats me on the shoulder, and my secretary
takes it in shorthand, and everywhere
efficiency doubles, I'm doing it, after all,
for them. And yet,
deep down, I know, in fact,
it's no more daffodils than it's half-soles—
what it really is,
is morning without a hangover
but an even chance of rain,
it's a cost-of-living raise
and a slight case of heartburn; well,
we all know about
the slow leak, the scratch
on our favorite record,
the 7:12 forty minutes late, sure—

194●

but passenger pigeons? Studebakers? That's
going too far,
we have our pride, our good
intentions, our metabolism, we won't
be shunted off with clipper ships
and whooping cranes, we're going
to hang in there, all of us, because
the robins may be showing wear,
but still, by god,
they are robins.

Philip Appleman

AFTER VAN GOGH

arms full of iris
she opens the door
with her backside

Raymond Roseliep

ACKNOWLEDGMENTS

All poems not listed hereunder are printed in *Light Year '85* for the first time; copyright remains vested in the poets. The following poems, previously copyrighted, are reprinted by permission of their authors or as otherwise indicated.

Katharyn Machan Aal. "Hazel Tells Laverne": © 1981 by Katharyn Machan Aal. First appeared in *Rapscallion's Dream* (vol. 1).

Dick Allen. "Young Poet's Lament": © 1982 by Dick Allen. First appeared in *Cutbank*. Reprinted from *Overnight in the Guest House of the Mystic* (Louisiana State University Press, 1984).

Philip Appleman. "The Trickle-Down Theory of Happiness": © 1983 by Philip Appleman. First appeared in *Poetry*. "Mr. Extinction, Meet Ms. Survival": © 1978 by Philip Appleman. First appeared in *Poetry*; forthcoming in *Darwin's Ark* (Indiana University Press).

R Bartkowech. "Fascism": © 1979 by R Bartkowech. First appeared in *Ten Point Five (Or) #8*.

Margaret Blaker. "A Good Mantra Is Hard to Find": © 1983 by Margaret C. Blaker. "Pippa Passes . . .": © 1982 by Margaret C. Blaker.

Alec Bond. "Birchers": © 1983 by Alec Bond. First appeared in *Spoon River Quarterly*. Reprinted from *North of Sioux Falls* (Hilary Press, 1983).

James Camp. "After the Philharmonic": © 1978 by James Camp. First appeared in *Open Places*.

William Cole. "Some River Rhymes": © 1983, 1984 by William Cole. Several first appeared in *The New York Times*.

Wendy Cope. "Strugnell's Bargain": © 1984 by Wendy Cope. First published by The Poetry Society. "A Policeman's Lot": © 1983 by Wendy Cope. First appeared in *Poetry Review* (UK) and *The Agni Review* (USA).

Wesli Court. "The Cat, the Maid, and the Gentleman": © 1983 by Wesli Court. First appeared in *Phantasm*.

Tom Disch. "Remaindered Titles at Barnes & Noble": © 1983 by Tom Disch. First appeared in *Amazing SF*.

Gavin Ewart. "Lexicography": © 1983 by Gavin Ewart. First appeared in *Maledicta*. " 'Came Away with Betjeman . . .' ": © 1983 by Gavin Ewart. First appeared in *Times Literary Supplement*.

James Facos. "Fable": © 1970 by James Facos. First appeared in *The Mountain Troubadour*.

Robert N. Feinstein. "The Owl": © 1983 by Robert N. Feinstein. First appeared in *The Lyric*.

Frederick Feirstein. "L'Art": © 1973 by Frederick Feirstein. First appeared in *Counter/Measures*.

Dana Gioia. "My Confessional Sestina": © 1983 by Dana Gioia. First appeared in *Poetry*.

Richard Goldsmith. "Epitaph for a Stripper": © 1974 by Richard Goldsmith. Reprinted from *Another Garland for Eve* (Shiver Mountain Press).

Raymond Griffith. "Ferns": © 1983 by Raymond Griffith. First appeared in *Windfall*. "Essay on Enjambment": © 1979 by Raymond Griffith. First appeared in *College Composition and Communication*.

Donald Hall. "Four Epigrams": © 1978, 1983 by Donald Hall. "On a Teacher" and "On a Philosopher" first appeared in *Poetry*, "On a Poet" and "On a Scholar" in *Sewanee Review*. Reprinted from *Brief Lives* (William B. Ewert, Publisher, Concord, New Hampshire, 1983).

William Harmon. "Caesarean Section": © 1982 by William Harmon. First appeared in *Children's Literature*. "Intertextuality": © 1983 by William Harmon. First appeared in *Sewanee Review*.

Ron Ikan. "Nightgame": © 1980 by Ron Ikan. First appeared in *Poetry Now*.

Phyllis Janowitz. "My Sister": © 1982 by Phyllis Janowitz. First appeared in *Ithaca Women's Anthology #7*. "Fat Lena and Mr. M.": © 1976 by Phyllis Janowitz. First appeared in *Lake Superior Review*.

Judson Jerome. "Shall I Compare Thee to Thy Aston Martin?": © 1979 by Judson Jerome. Reprinted from *Thirty Years of Poetry* (Collected Poems: 1949–1979), Cedar Rock Press.

A. L. Lazarus. "Traveler's Agent": © 1966 by A. L. Lazarus. First appeared in *Massachusetts Review*. "Kalispera": © 1969 by A. L. Lazarus. First appeared in *The New Republic*.

Dan Masterson. "The Outing": © 1977 by Dan Masterson. First appeared in *Poetry*. Reprinted from *On Earth As It Is* (Illinois University Press).

Gloria Maxson. "Candidate": © 1983 by Gloria A. Maxson. First appeared in *National Review*.

Richard Moore. "On Coming to Nothing": © 1981 by Richard Moore. First appeared in *Poetry*.

Howard Nemerov. "Disseverings, Divorces," "Death of a Virgin," "Morality," "Imprecated upon a Postal Clerk": © 1984 by Howard Nemerov. Reprinted from *Inside the Onion* (University of Chicago Press, 1984).

Kirby Olson. "A Kirby Olson Adventure Canzone": © 1983 by Kirby Olson. First appeared in *Uncle*.

Louis Phillips. From "The Big City Mother Goose": © 1983 by Louis Phillips.

Marge Piercy. "If I had been called Sabrina or Ann, she said": © 1981 by Marge Piercy. "The maternal instinct at work": © 1983 by Marge Piercy.

F. C. Rosenberger. "Poets Observed": © 1978 by F. C. Rosenberger. "On the Economics of Publishing Poetry": © 1977 by F. C. Rosenberger. Both first appeared in *Arizona Quarterly* and are reprinted from *An Alphabet* (University Press of Virginia, 1978).

Larry Rubin. "A Note on Library Policy": © 1962 by Larry Rubin. First appeared in *The Colorado Quarterly*. Reprinted from *The World's Old Way*.

Delmore Schwartz. "Exercise in Preparation for a Pindaric Ode to Carl Hubbell," "All Poets' Wives Have Rotten Lives," "A Wise Question," "Letter to Oranges": © 1984 by Robert Phillips, Literary Executor for the Estate of Delmore Schwartz.

Judith Skillman. "Behind an RV": © 1984 by Judith Skillman. First appeared in *New Jersey Poetry Review*.

INDEX OF POETS